Review

"YOUR SON DID NOT DIE IN VAIN!"

Liz Woolley gives a heartbreaking account of the story of her son Shawn that every mother of a gamer should read. She has captured the darkness of gaming addiction and the details that are missing in our cultural conversation about this issue. My favorite quote from this heartfelt book is, *"Every mom has a mission. To love, guide and protect her family. Don't mess with her while she is on it."* (Vicki Reece) Thank you Liz for using your insight and God-given strength to write a painful but clear warning to all parents of gamers. This book will save lives.

Melanie Hempe, BSN
Executive Director | Families Managing Media
Author of "The Screen Strong Solution."

This is a book every American should read. It tells of the massive entertainment industry's greed-fueled assault on our children, which has spawned a public health and public safety crisis.

Jack Thompson
Author of "Out of Harm's Way"

Our rapidly evolving technology offers us an opportunity to work, play, and relate to each other in novel ways. It can, however come at a cost. This important story of a mother and her son highlights how in our current world our vulnerabilities and the way that technology can activate those vulnerabilities can lead us down a path away from wellness and towards more suffering. This is a must read for parents of children, teens and emerging adults.

Mathew Meyers, MA, LMFT
Therapist and Owner of Traverse Counseling & Consulting

I began studying video game "addiction" in 1999 because I believed all of the talk about it was hyperbole. Twenty years later we find that there are some people for whom this term is appropriate. Hopefully the story of Shawn can help families recognize the symptoms so that people can get the help they deserve.
Douglas A. Gentile, PhD
Research on the Effects of Media
Author of "Media Violence and Children"

1

The World Health Organization recognizes video game addiction as a mental disorder. With the inclusion of "Gaming Disorder" into the International Statistical Classification of Diseases and Related Health Problems, or ICD-11, this book is an important work. Woolley's book about her son's journey into the dark depths of gaming disorder is a heartbreaking account and analysis of the progression from normal to full-blown addiction. This book provides insight into the minds of gamers.

Andrew Doan, MD, PhD
Author of "Hooked on Games", "Digital Vortex Survival Guide",
and numerous peer-reviewed articles on video game addiction.

I was particularly touched by the way Liz Woolley has told the story as a mother, friend and advocate, of her late son Shawn. She has melded together all facets of life -- at the forefront spiritual, but also medical, scientific, emotional, personal, familial, relationships, daily life, business, work, growing up .... It is a hope that others can benefit from the insight gained through this trauma, and that they may be rescued from the same path. Even though I helped break the newspaper story, almost two decades ago, Liz has told that story far better than I ever could, by putting a personal, motherly, extremely caring and human face on what is a huge problem that is not being addressed. So much has occurred since then that is vital for so many people to know. Despite all of the horrific strife she has been through, Liz keeps a positive and upbeat attitude -- no easy task. I would like to think that Shawn is looking down from Heaven and smiling in approval of what his mom is doing via things such as this book. Take care friends, both of you. I would highly recommend this book to anybody.

Joe Winter
Free-lance writer for various types of publications across the Midwest.
Specializing in medical and religious topics.

This is a really heart-rending story, movingly told. You can become addicted to a lot more than drugs and alcohol - and we need to think more deeply and intelligently about behavioral addictions. This book is a great place to start.

Johann Hari
Author of "Lost Connections"

Even after having Liz as a dear friend for many years and knowing her story well, I am still shocked having read this detailed account... Addictions manifest in a myriad of forms, but the most insidious are the socially acceptable ones. Although not every family will have their lives altered as tragically as the Woolley family, the effects of gaming addiction are serious and devastate families worldwide. Thank you Liz, for being so bold, and helping so many.

Mike Taratuta
Enterprise Software Architect
Vice President of Board of Director of On-Line Gamers Anonymous®
World Services

As a pediatric and adolescent psychologist, I have come to appreciate that video game addiction is an epidemic problem. There is an emerging body of research, which bears evidence that the lives of our young people are being tragically altered and diminished by excessive media consumption. *Your Son Did Not Die in Vain* does a masterful job of sharing Shawn's tragic story of his decent into media addiction and subsequent suicide. This important work helps us appreciate how dangerous certain forms of excessive gaming can be. It is my hope that the reader will be enlightened to the threat of this behavioral addiction. Shawn's moving story will serve as a warning to the reader of the serious need for discernment in the specific choice of media engaged in as well as balance in the amount of time spent consuming it.

Jeffrey E. Hansen, PhD
Staff Pediatric and Adolescent Psychologist, Madigan Army Medical Center

YOUR SON DID

NOT

DIE IN VAIN!

A true story about the devastating effects of video gaming addiction.

YOUR SON DID NOT DIE IN VAIN!

A true story about the devastating effects of video gaming addiction.

Written by Liz Woolley
With John M. Langel, Sr.

Table of Contents

Dedication

This book is dedicated to the first addicted video gamer I knew, my son, Shawn, may he rest in peace.

To my living children who I love and cherish – Ryan, Crystal and Tony.

To my friend John, if it were not for him, this book would still be on my computer.

To Shawn's godparents, Maureen Stock and Chuck Wulf, and Shawn's grandma, Vera Wulf, may you all rest in peace! Thank you for your love, support and encouragement of Shawn on his spiritual journey. You are now all up in heaven with Shawn. May you rejoice eternally and support us on our mission!

To God, may He receive all of the glory, honor and praise.

Preface

YOUR SON DID NOT DIE IN VAIN! Is the biography of Shawn Woolley, written by his mother Liz. Shawn who was addicted to the online video game Everquest took his own life in November 2001. As a result, in 2002 Liz founded *On-Line Gamers Anonymous®* (OLGA), www.olganon.org, a 12-step self-help group. OLGA's goal is **"Sharing our experience, strength and hope to support each other to recover from problems resulting from excessive video game playing"** (commonly called gaming disorder).

This book is both troubling and an inspiration to those struggling with many forms of addiction. The book's title comes from a response to a message Liz had posted on the internet. The reply was from a person who benefitted from hearing her story.

Liz, ***Your son did NOT die in vain!***

On a personal level: I am the mother of a son (21) who almost died due to health problems because of the game. I don't post often, and it's been a long time, but awhile back I posted with an update for those who knew his story. He's now in the Marines training to be an MP. He joined the USMC, before we knew about your son, out of desperation because his life was falling apart into an Everquest Black Hole.

When he came home on leave after graduating from boot camp, we discussed your tragedy. He actually cried in front of me, and then went to his room. I walked by a few minutes later and he was praying, thanking God for helping him get back to the real world, praying for his friends still addicted to Everquest, and praying for your son. He started going to church in Boot Camp, and I didn't even know!

So, now he is starting his new real-life adventure. And without a look back to the fantasy life he led, and rest assured, your son helped him to do this. My prayers are with you, and my heart-felt sympathies and appreciation.

Terri

Forward by John M. Langel Sr.

Do you like going to the movies? I don't mean for the popcorn and extra butter! I don't even mean for the extra treats or a night away from the children. I mean to go to the movies for the experience and to learn something new about history, people, or an event. I love going to the movies and on Saturday, February 10, 2018 I had a life-changing experience. In the morning, I was participating in a Nikken meeting for an upcoming event that we were sponsoring in the Harrisburg, PA area. We were promoting wellness and encouraging people to take the initiative of how self-care is the best health care. One of the other members of the planning team was a lady by the name of Liz Woolley. This was the first time I had ever met her. Liz shared she had been with Nikken for about 4 years. She was very engaged in the meeting with suggestions and insights. Liz shared different stories about her experiences using Nikken products. After the meeting, we talked some more and laughed about some different experiences in our lives. Later that afternoon, I called Liz to ask her if she likes going to the movies. She said yes, if it is a good movie. I shared with Liz about a film that was called Winchester. This motion picture is based on a true story about the gun manufacturer and I wondered if she would be interested in seeing it with me? Liz said she had heard of the film and wanted to see the show herself so we made plans to go see Winchester that night.

WOW! What a show! I'm not sure I was ready to deal with all the nonsense, and twisted horror, in this fascinating, real-life story. I just kept wondering where this flick was going and what was its message. How did this movie apply to my life? Then, towards the end, I started wondering what Liz thought of all this confusion – death and demons/spirits. As the film finally ended, and we sat there watching the credits on the big screen and people leaving to go home, Liz turned to me and said the most bizarre, unthinkable sentence I believe I ever heard after a movie. I was just sitting in my seat, dazed in my heart and mind, trying to make some kind of sense of the nonsense I had just experienced for the last two hours. Then Liz blows my world upside down and inside out when she turns to me, looks me directly in the eye, and says, "my son died by suicide." What? What are you talking about? Now the motion picture was inconsequential. How am I going to respond to this NEW piece of information?

I was trying desperately to absorb the impact of her words and wondering what kind of sick joke God was playing in my life. I just watched a film that was disturbing to my spirit, heart and mind and the lady I am with for the FIRST time shares a terrible, tragic experience about one of her children. Now my heart and mind are blown worlds apart. Then Liz shares, "my son killed himself with a rifle, but it wasn't a Winchester." What is this lady talking about? Where is she coming from? Why would someone share that information with a person they just met during their first time together? I just wanted to get up and run out of the movie theater and try to forget what I just experienced. This whole experience was just too bizarre for me to handle. It was like living in an episode of the Twilight Zone. As we sat in silence next to each other – wondering who was going to talk next – my mind and heart began to function again and I was flooded with a thousand questions. For the next two hours, we talked about Liz's life and began our journey together of uncovering the reason God had us together at this motion picture. The more questions I had, the more answers Liz shared, the clearer our purpose became. I could not believe the gentleness, kindness, transparency, and humility in Liz's answers to all of my questions. I asked when and where and how and why did her son, Shawn, take his life. Liz shared with me how on Thanksgiving morning of 2001, she found her son Shawn in his apartment, dead.

Every question I asked raised another three questions. Liz shared with me how Shawn's death was from an addiction to a video computer game called Everquest. As I listened to Liz answer my questions, I became more aware of the incredible compassion this lady has for life and people. As a result of her son Shawn's death, Liz then shared that she had started a 12-step organization called On-Line Gamers Anonymous® (OLGA/OLG-Anon/Outreach) to support people who are affected by video game addiction. This organization was way out of my league. I had experienced the devastating effects of alcoholism, drug addiction, gambling, and pornography, yet knew nothing of video game addiction or the terrible, incredible effects on people's lives and their families around the world.

I finally asked THE burning question in my mind. I asked Liz "have you ever considered writing a book?" She immediately responded, saying, "It is already written". I said WHAT? May I read it? Liz shared that it has not been published yet. I asked, "May I help you do that?" We both agreed to start the journey of sharing Liz's life experience of Shawn's tragedy and the purpose and vision and mission of On-Line Gamers Anonymous® (OLGA/OLG-Anon/Outreach). It truly has been an honor and a blessing to listen and ask questions and share this story so her son, Shawn, did not die in vain. Charlie "Tremendous" Jones often said, "Remember, you are the same today as you will be in five years, except for two things: the people you meet and the books you read. Choose both carefully." My life has been drastically improved, changed, and blessed by meeting and working with Liz Woolley and her family. May the Holy Spirit use these words to encourage and challenge you in your life's journey. Get ready to experience the wild and CRAZY ride!

Thankfully,

John M. Langel Sr.

Executive Director of Outreach for On-Line Gamers Anonymous®

www.olganon.org

Acknowledgements

I wrote this book as a true testament of what I saw happen to my son, Shawn, after he became addicted to the Everquest video game. There have been some articles and videos done about him with half-truths and slanted opinions. This book tells what really happened.

This book is being released in conjunction with the revolutionary milestone of the World Health Organization (WHO) recognizing video game addiction as a mental disorder. These two events are *God-incidental* (as quoted on July 9 of "Letting God" by A. Philip Parham.) It is my wish that this book encourage the American Psychiatric Association (APA) to include video game addiction as a diagnosis in the Diagnostic Statistical Manual of Mental Disorders (DSM) making it a recognized health risk in the United States. This will allow insurance companies to pay for treatment for those looking for and needing help for video game addiction/disorder.

I would like to express my appreciation to my mom and dad for getting me to adulthood alive. Both my parents provided structure and encouragement of a Godly foundation in my life. This structure provided for the significance and importance of having an awareness and relationship with God.

To Shawn's oldest brother, Ryan, who watched over him and helped keep Shawn out of trouble when they went on their excursions together, thank you. I would also like to say thank you for providing a positive, wholesome, responsible example for Shawn as his older brother. You finished what you started, did your homework, were a hard worker and God-fearing. You were a loving, caring older brother. You laughed with him and endured Shawn's wacky sense of humor.

To Shawn's only sister, Crystal, I'd like say thank you for loving Shawn unconditionally and for always being there for him. As Ryan was, you were also a responsible, hardworking, finish what you started, role model for him. Crystal, you were a great example of kindness and sensitivity for Shawn. You were an excellent role model for Shawn with your love for animals, especially for the cats.

To Tony, Shawn's baby brother, thank you for your loving, kind, and peace-making attitude toward Shawn. Thanks for being Shawn's playful, fun-loving younger brother and for keeping us entertained with your "in-the-driveway" and "on-the-road" sports play. Thank you for sharing everything that you had with Shawn. You held nothing back. You were a real friend to him.

To all of my children, thank you for being such a wonderful, supportive family of whom I am deeply proud to be a part of.

I would like to acknowledge and thank Mike Stock, Shawn's cousin, for his kindness to Shawn and for being his protector while he was on this earth. Shawn was probably closest to him of all of his cousins, as he was the same age and they hung out together. Thank you for being there for him.

I would like to thank Greg Woolley and Elaine Duncan for their caring for Shawn when he was growing up. Thank you for taking him on vacations, special outings and for making him feel wanted, needed, loved and part of a family. Also thank you for your encouragement and support in the years after Shawn's death with the On-Line Gamers Anonymous® organization.

To my brothers and sisters, aunts and uncles, nieces and nephews, in-laws and out-laws, thank you for all of your support and encouragement over these years as I struggle to find healing in this grieving process.

I would like to voice my appreciation to Mike Taratuta, with whom I have shared my mission and vision of On-Line Gamers Anonymous®, since 2004. Thank you for your continued support, encouragement, cheering on and boosting up, when I needed it the most. Thank you for your input and contributions to our cause (and offering support to those affected by excessive video gaming) as you have experienced it first-hand.

A special thank you to my niece Heather Kelly, who has spent countless hours proofreading and editing this book. Thank you for your many suggestions for improvement of the book and for your faithfulness to this project and the OLGA/OLG-Anon/Outreach organization.

We are truly grateful for the many hands and hearts that have made this book possible. We love and appreciate you all!

And one final thank you to the Giver of all words, our Heavenly Father, Jesus Christ and the Holy Spirit. Would you convince the ones who read these words that REAL life is WORTH LIVING?

Gratefully,
Liz Woolley
Founder of On-Line Gamers Anonymous®
www.olganon.org

Introduction

This poem was on a sympathy card my family had received when my dad died in 1995. I saved the card because it touched my heart.

The Plan of the Master Weaver

Our lives are but fine weavings that God and we prepare,
Each life becomes a fabric planned and fashioned in His care...
We may not always see just how the weavings intertwine,
But we must trust the Master's hand and follow His design,
For He can view the pattern upon the upper side,
While we must look from underneath and trust in Him to guide...
Sometimes a strand of sorrow is added to His plan,
And though it's difficult for us, we still must understand,
That it's He who fills the shuttle; it's He, who knows what's best,
So we must weave in patience and leave to Him the rest...
Not till the loom is silent and the shuttles cease to fly
Shall God unroll the canvas and explain the reason why—
The dark threads are as needed in the Weaver's skillful hand
As the threads of gold and silver in the pattern He has planned.
Author unknown.

My son Shawn, died and now I have dark threads, the strands of sorrow in my pattern. I will see my whole picture after I die.

Several years after my father passed away, I discovered a Christian devotional book for those in recovery. It soon became one of my favorite books. It is titled: "Letting God" by A. Philip Parham. After reading the book daily for many years I was enlightened to the reading of November 7, which happens to be my dad's birthday. The following is quoted from that reading:

"For now we see in a mirror, dimly, but then face-to-face.
Now I know in part; then I shall understand fully,
Even as I have been fully understood. 1 Corinthians 13:12

More often than we would like, we are puzzled and perplexed by our troubles. So much of our difficulty seems senseless. When our troubles don't make any sense, we can remember these words.

"Not till the loom is silent and the shuttles cease to fly
Shall God unroll the canvas and explain the reason why."

When everything seems futile and senseless, we see from our perspective, not God's. We can see only confusion. God sees purpose and plan; He is in control and directing the action. We can eliminate more confusion by relaxing and trusting His supervision. He knows where He's going, and He knows where He's going with us.

A woman experienced a sudden and apparently senseless tragedy. She was so crushed that she said in her sorrow, "I wish that I had never been made." Her friend said, "My dear, you are not yet made. You're only being made. God is not finished with you yet." We are all on God's loom. He is weaving us. The rough and dark threads combine with the smooth and light ones to produce what He has in mind."

I was stunned that I had not noticed the reference this reading had to the poem, The Plan of the Master Weaver, from the sympathy card for my dad that we had received many years before! A message, a gift, a *God-incident*, a feeling of relief, that yes, there is a God and we will be with Him and our loved ones again!

The sorrow of losing a child will always be there. After all these years I have a different perspective now. It is not so much about my son, Shawn. It is about reaching out and helping others.

Today when I get emails or phone calls, or read an article or hear on the nightly news about another tragic mass shooting, I grieve for the other mothers, the other parents, the other family members, the other video gamers who are now going through what we went through. There is still no diagnosis for video gaming addiction or disorder in the DSM (Diagnostic Statistical Manual of Mental Disorders) making it an unrecognized health risk in the United States. Therefore insurance companies are not required to pay for treatment. What is happening with the video gaming and technology addictions is preventable or curable, with the right help and support, IF people can afford it!

Will you join us in the fight to get help for video gamers, for their family members, for our society as a whole, to end these senseless tragedies? This needs to be a worldwide movement because of the damage these video games and technology are doing to our brains, our bodies, our spirits, our hearts and minds and our society. We'd love to have you join the movement,

"Gaming is your business... Quitting is ours!"

Chapter 1: Let The Games Begin

To hear your own soul you must have the sound of silence.
Anonymous

There was a time when silence was normal, acceptable and cherished. Today, this is a noisy world – the world of cell phones, video games, I-pods, I-pads, tablets, television, power tools and vehicles which surround us in a constant cacophony. We can't even make a telephone call and be put on hold in silence. Music has been added! Now we must put forth conscious effort to create silence so that we may be able to listen to the whispering voice of peace or the first cry of a newborn baby.

On Tuesday, February 12, 1980 around 2:00 a.m. I gave birth to Shawn Paul Beer (Woolley) in the hospital at St. Croix Falls, WI. He weighed 8 lbs. 1 oz. and was 21" long. Shawn was my third child. His brother Ryan was four years old, and his sister Crystal was two years old at the time. Seven years later my last child, Tony would be added to our family.

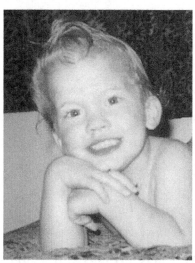

Shawn at 18 months old.

Here are some very special people in Shawn's life. I chose my twin brother, Chuck Wulf, and my younger sister, Maureen Stock, as Shawn's godparents. They were very positive role models in Shawn's life. They came to his birthday parties and we celebrated major holidays together. Maureen's son, Mike, was the same age as Shawn. They grew up together and were best buddies. They went to public school together, played baseball and basketball together, went to confirmation class and graduated from Osceola High School in 1998 together.

Shawn's first birthday with godparents.

Shawn was a healthy baby. He wasn't sick and he slept well. He laughed a lot and was very good humored and easy going. Shawn got along with everyone. He was always trying to keep up with his older brother, Ryan, and sister, Crystal. Shawn was very active and liked to show off. He liked being outside and could sit there playing for hours. Shawn liked getting attention from everyone.

We had a family tradition. When it was someone's birthday and we made a birthday cake, the person whose birthday it was got to be special and lick out the cake bowl.

Shawn's 2nd birthday. Licking out the cake bowl!

One of the special times in Shawn's early childhood was being in the wedding of his babysitter. His brother, Ryan, was the ring bearer. His sister, Crystal, was the flower girl and he was the junior attendant. There was a dance after the wedding. Shawn had a great time dancing with everyone!

Crystal, Ryan and Shawn at babysitter's wedding in 1983.

⏺ In 1985, when Shawn was 5 years old, I received my associate's degree in Computer Programming and Operations from 916 Vocational School (now called Century College) in White Bear Lake, MN. I got my first job as a computer programmer at the Hazelden Alcoholic Treatment Center in Center City, MN. We moved from Hudson to Osceola, WI. We now lived only two blocks away from my mother, Vera Wulf. We visited her often. She was a tremendous help to us. She liked to have the children come over and visit with her. She went to their T-Ball games. Sometimes she would babysit for them while I was working, and helped in many other ways.

Shawn's 5th birthday party.

On July 29, 1985 Shawn started having grand mal seizures. He had his first seizure on my birthday when he was at his daycare center. This was just the beginning of this life-long health disorder. After many trips to the neurologist, chiropractor, and family doctor Shawn was diagnosed with epilepsy. I was terrified and perplexed about what to do and how to help my young son. I was a struggling, single mother with 3 young children and was now faced with this major medical condition. Over the next year and 8 months Shawn had 20 seizures, many appointments with several doctors and was on several different medications in an attempt to control his seizures. Finally, in February of 1987 our local physician, Dr. Mark Boyken, prescribed Depakote for Shawn. This medication worked wonderfully at controlling Shawn's seizures. Shawn was seizure-free for the next 13 years, until he started playing video games excessively in the year 2000.

In 1986 when Shawn was in first grade, he joined Cub Scouts. Shawn enjoyed interacting with the other boys, and learning while he earned his badges Later, Shawn advanced to the Boy Scouts and continued learning about life and character building.

On May 30 of 1987, I married Greg Woolley. We had a beautiful outdoor wedding at my house. It was a small, close family ceremony. Shawn always wanted to have a dad. Greg, his new stepdad, finally filled that emotional need in Shawn's life. Shawn was happy and so was I. Shawn wanted his last name changed to Woolley. In 1988 we changed Shawn's last name from Beer to Woolley, so the connection was complete. Shawn felt like he fully belonged in our family. It was official! Now Shawn had a mom AND a dad.

Shawn's new stepdad, Greg (L), brother Ryan and Shawn (R).

Another exciting event in the Beer-Woolley household happened later that year. On November 24, 1987 Shawn welcomed a new baby brother, Tony, into our family. Shawn loved the idea of having a younger brother so he would not be the youngest child in the family.

1987 Family photo.
(L to R) Ryan, Liz, Tony, Greg, Shawn, Crystal.

In 1989 at the age of 9, Shawn became an altar boy for the St. Joseph Catholic Church in Osceola. He often went to weekday masses with his Grandma Vera and served at those masses. Shawn enjoyed being helpful while in front of the congregation rather than sitting in the front pew being bored.

That same year an incredible tragedy occurred three days before Christmas. The house we were living in caught on fire from faulty electrical wiring in the attic. Fortunately, Shawn's little brother, Tony, woke up crying in the middle of the night because his finger was hurting. When I got up to soothe Tony, I heard crackling up by the ceiling in the master bedroom. I asked my husband, Greg, to go up into the attic to see what was causing that crackling sound. Greg went up into the attic and saw flames in the rafters and yelled for everyone to get out of the house. We quickly called the fire department and took the children over to my mom's house. The second floor of our house was pretty much destroyed.

Two separate fires cause extensive damage to home in Osceola

Osceola Fire Chief Bill Lones reported that while electricity was the probable cause of two fires on Friday, December 22, they were separate places of origin.

The Osceola Fire Department was first called to the Greg Woolley residence at 614 Summit Street, Osceola, at approximately 2:12 a.m. It was reported that the attic was full of smoke. According to Lones insulation in the attic had been ignited by faulty wiring, or that was the probable cause.

The Woolley residence was again reported on fire at approximately 6:30 a.m. that same day. According to Lones, when the firefighters arrived the front bedroom at 614 Summit was engulfed in flames. Again electricity was believed to be the cause of this fire.

Lones stressed that the two fires on Friday had separate places of origin. The second fire at the Woolley residence forced the family to leave the home. Lones reports that the structure is definitely repairable.

1989 This is what our home looked like after the Christmas fire.

We rented an empty house in town and lived there for the next several months. We missed Christmas that year. The Christmas gifts that were stored on the second floor were destroyed. We later had our own "belated" Christmas in February. Because of the fire, there was a lot of turmoil, noise and confusion going on in our family life and a lot of transition. Greg's mom, Grace, also moved in with us at this time. After the house was rebuilt from the fire, we sold the house and moved back to Hudson, WI.

At the new house Shawn attended the St. Patrick Catholic School. Shawn was now 10 years old and in fifth grade. He liked music and was very talented. Shawn decided he wanted to learn to play a musical instrument. He chose the saxophone and started taking private lessons from Ruth Ashwood at St. Patrick's school.

Shawn decided to join the school band and then eventually the marching band. He played in the marching band at neighboring events during the summer. He played at Booster Days in Hudson, WI and at Pepper Fest days in North Hudson, WI. Shawn was soon able to transfer this music skill over to playing the trumpet.

Things were getting rocky on the home front for the Woolley couple. Due to a major, unfortunate incident, Greg and I split up. Greg left our home in October of 1990. This was a very sad and stressful time for our family. Our divorce was final in June of 1991.

Because of the loss of income in our household, we could no longer stay in our home, and had to move to a rental property. I could no longer afford to send Shawn to the private Catholic school. I transferred him to the Hudson Middle School beginning in the fall of 1991. Shawn was in 6th grade. This was the biggest public school Shawn had ever attended. Shawn was a good student. He did well academically, got along with his classmates and his teachers appreciated him. See **Appendix A: Sample of Shawn's work.** Shawn was very sensitive toward his classmates and other people.

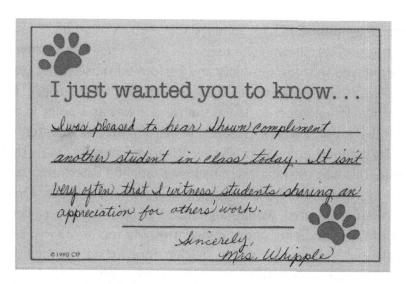

I just wanted you to know...

I was pleased to hear Shawn compliment another student in class today. It isn't very often that I witness students sharing an appreciation for others' work.

Sincerely,
Mrs. Whipple

© 1990 CTP

Shawn received this note from his sixth grade teacher at the Hudson Middle School.

On Christmas day in 1991 when Shawn was 11 years old we went to his Aunt Maggie and his Uncle Chuck's home to celebrate Christmas. Almost my whole family – my mom, my brothers and sisters and their spouses, and children were there. There was a lot of snow on the ground. The children were outside playing in the snow and happily sledding. Some of the adults were watching as the children were going down the big hill on their sleds. There was only one tree on the entire hill. Shawn was heading straight for the tree. We all started screaming at the top of our lungs, "Don't hit the tree, don't hit the tree!" Shawn barreled into the tree feet first! We ran down to see if he was okay. Shawn couldn't walk. Several of the dads carried Shawn to the car. I took him to the emergency room at the hospital in Stillwater, MN. The hospital was pretty quiet because most people were at home celebrating Christmas. After the doctor ordered x-rays, he concluded that Shawn had broken his ankle. We spent the afternoon there while they put a cast on his leg. This made for another interesting Christmas.

We all went to church on Sundays at St. Patrick's Catholic Church in Hudson, WI. Shawn volunteered as an altar boy there, as well. He enjoyed that responsibility and performed those duties well. Shawn attended catechism class on Wednesday evenings. No one would volunteer to teach the class. I was at a point in my spiritual journey where I stepped in out of faith and volunteered to be the teacher for Shawn's seventh grade catechism class that year. This was the first time I had ever taught a catechism class. On average there were about 20 students in the class. I was nervous and scared, wondering if I was going to be able to keep all of those students under my control. My top priority was to make sure they had a healthy snack before we started the class so they could concentrate on what I was going to teach them. I enjoyed teaching the boys and girls how to make their faith real to them. I encouraged the students to have fun and to be creative. Shawn learned and blossomed in his faith and social skills in this safe environment. He became more confident with himself and was able to practice his faith while interacting with the other students. He reached out and shared with more of the students. We were like a community rather than a classroom.

In 1992, while in 7th grade Shawn was having trouble focusing at his new, larger public school and his grades were declining. I was very concerned for Shawn. He was a smart, gifted, sensitive, talented child. Now he was not as happy and he was getting lower grades. We went to see a therapist. Shawn was diagnosed with ADD. The therapist prescribed Cylert for his ADD. The two medications (Depakote for his seizures and Cylert for his ADD) worked well together for Shawn. We were relieved. Shawn was able to concentrate better and his grades improved. Shawn was also entering that danger zone of puberty. His body was starting to go through physical changes and his brain was going through emotional changes. The large school classes were still overwhelming for Shawn. He was still having a hard time making friends because there were so many students. Plus there was not as much adult interaction or supervision in his new school.

Shawn's school picture when he was 12 (7th grade).

1993 Shawn (R) and his brother Tony (L) on a pontoon boat with his stepdad, Greg on the St. Croix River.

When Shawn was 13, he went on a trip to Washington D.C. with his stepdad, Greg, Greg's girlfriend, Elaine, and his younger brother, Tony. They stayed there for 4 days and saw historic landmarks. Greg shared this about Shawn and their vacation: *"I remember how thrilled he was about his first airplane flight. We went to Washington D.C. and took in all the sights. I think he liked the capital building the best."* Shawn was super excited to have been able to go to visit the capital of our country. It was a trip that he would never forget.

September 1993, Shawn and his brother Tony lying on floor of the rotunda at the capitol building in Washington D.C. while on vacation with stepdad Greg and Elaine.

This concludes the first level of Shawn's real life. In the chapters ahead, we will see how Shawn does with the competition in the next level of his real life.

Chapter 2: Leveling Up (or Down)

"Though we travel the world over to find the beautiful, we must carry it with us or we find it not." Ralph Waldo Emerson

In October 1993, I took a new job at Phillips Plastics in New Richmond, WI. I decided it would be best for our family and the children to move back to Osceola, WI. The house was close to my mother and we were already familiar with the town. Plus we knew the people there. I knew they had a great school district. Shawn was glad we moved back to the smaller school. He did much better socially and academically.

Shawn continued his music, playing the trumpet and saxophone in the Osceola school and marching bands. He played at the yearly Wheel's and Wings event in Osceola, WI. Shawn was in band until he got his first job at age 15 at Hardees.

Shawn playing trumpet in the Osceola High School marching band.

As a mother and fan of the Green Bay Packers, I knew Shawn definitely had some issues when he became a Dallas Cowboy fan! It was a most "traumatic" experience to find that Shawn's stepdad had given him this Dallas Cowboy bath towel for Christmas. Because I loved my son so much I allowed him to bring it into our house. (Ha, ha, ha!)

Christmas 1994 - Cowboy fan in Packer country. Awesome Christmas gift from stepdad Greg.

Shawn was a sensitive person. He was not competitive athletically. Shawn enjoyed sports just for the fun of it. Shawn loved art and he was very good at it. He was quite creative with his art and writing. He was funny. He had a dry sense of humor. Shawn reminded me a lot of Jim Carrey, goofy and funny. He could mimic Mr. Carey very well. He also liked the humor of comedian Steve Martin. Shawn liked to make people laugh. He just wanted people to like him.

Shawn's 15th birthday. Georgetown Hoyas hat, his favorite college basketball team.

Some of the other activities Shawn liked to do were painting, bowling, downhill snow skiing, roller skating, watching TV, riding his bike, playing his saxophone and trumpet. Favorite sports of Shawn's were baseball, basketball and football. He also liked going boating and fishing. At this time, some of the computer games that Shawn liked to play were: Doom, Doom II, Solitaire, Pacman, Cyberia and Mortal Kombat II.

Shawn liked to play and have fun. He was a kind and warm-hearted person. He was really good with children. He liked being a kid, with the kids. He felt more comfortable with the little ones, then with the judgmental, mean, adults. He could be himself and not be judged or condemned for it. He felt accepted with no pressure to perform.

Shawn had two cats at our home in Hudson, named George and Butternut. He loved his kitties.

This is how his cousin Joe Stock described him: *"If I was ever having a bad day and I saw Shawn, it was like the sun just broke through the clouds. I remember Shawn as **the** funniest person I knew."*

Below is a heart-breaking piece Shawn wrote for school, when he was 15, describing himself:

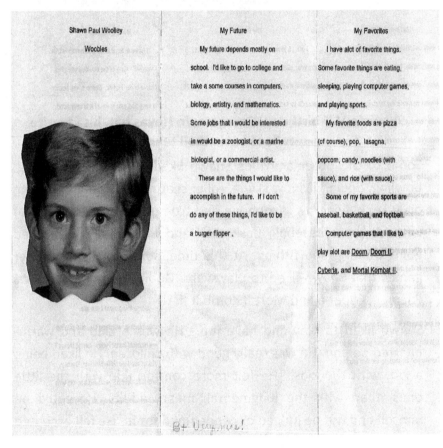

Shawn Paul Woolley

Woobles

My Future

My future depends mostly on school. I'd like to go to college and take a some courses in computers, biology, artistry, and mathematics.

Some jobs that I would be interested in would be a zoologist, or a marine biologist, or a commercial artist.

These are the things I would like to accomplish in the future. If I don't do any of these things, I'd like to be a burger flipper.

My Favorites

I have alot of favorite things. Some favorite things are eating, sleeping, playing computer games, and playing sports.

My favorite foods are pizza (of course), pop, lasagna, popcorn, candy, noodles (with sauce), and rice (with sauce).

Some of my favorite sports are baseball, basketball, and football.

Computer games that I like to play alot are Doom, Doom II, Cyberia, and Mortal Kombat II.

B+ Ury nice!

My Early Childhood

My early childhood was rough. If I wasn't getting into trouble, I would be crying cause I got hurt. Also, I moved alot, and I rarely had time to make friends because my mom always got a new job somewhere out of town and we had to move so she wouldn't have to travel very far. I went to many different schools, half of them were private and half of them public. Most of the kids at the schools I went had the same reaction as most of the people here at the Osceola High School. They all think because I act weird I'm stupid, or a moron, or an idiot, or any other neanderthalic name. People were always telling me to shutup when I say a couple of words, when they're the ones who should shutup. To summarize it all up, it would make me feel alot happier if I hadn't even existed. Of course, to the people who have been nice to me, I say, "Thanks alot for making me feel wanted."

The Basics

I am 15 years old. I was born on February 12, in the year 1980. I can't give you my exact weight because it's like a roller coaster, It ranges from 125 pounds to 145 pounds. My height is 6 feet without the shoes, and 6 feet 1 inch with the shoes. My eyes are hazel colored and my hair color is blonde.

Me in a Nutshell

I have at least three personalities that I know of. One of the obvious ones that I have is my humor. Some of my humor is very bad and some of it is very good. I don't its funny until the people around me laugh. Another personality that I have is my dramatic personality. I rarely show this personality because I only use it for plays. The only other one that I know of is my goofy personality. I use this one just as much as my humor, because I like to annoy annoying people. If you see any more just keep it to yourself.

Some things that I like are rollerblading, watching t.v., and playing my musical instruments. Some things I dislike are Pee Wee Herman, Barney, and men over 35 years old and flirt with women over two times as young as they are.

In the fall of 1995, Shawn got his first job at the local Hardees in Osceola, WI, at the age of 15. He decided to stop playing in the school band because of his job. Shawn shared with me that he really enjoyed playing music in the bands yet he enjoyed this new challenge of working and meeting new people. He looked forward to making money. Most of all he liked Hardee's food!

At that time Cal was the manager at Hardees. Here are some of the comments that Cal shared about Shawn: " *I interviewed Shawn for his job at Hardee's. He was about 15 years old. He was kind of shy but tried really hard to do the best he could. He wasn't very tall and he was skinny. Hardee's food must have*

37

agreed with him because he grew about 8 inches and gained about 100 pounds! He also "grew" into more responsibility, as he became a crew leader/supervisor in training. It was a pleasure to see Shawn grow BOTH ways!"

In November of 1995, we celebrated Shawn's younger brother Tony's 8th birthday at Hardee's. Tony's stepdad, Greg and Elaine, his sister Crystal, and several of the neighborhood children also participated. Shawn was the host. Shawn was a little nervous, as this was the first birthday party that he had hosted. He did a great job tending to everyone's needs to make sure all had a good time. Tony had a wonderful birthday party and everyone enjoyed themselves. I was a proud parent, watching Shawn perform his duties at his new job. Plus, it brought me great satisfaction to know that Tony had a tremendous birthday party.

Shawn hosting Tony's 8th birthday party at Hardees in 1995.

In the summer of 1996 when Shawn was 16 years old, he went on a ten-day vacation to South Dakota with his brother Tony, stepdad Greg, Elaine and Elaine's parents, Lucille and Bob. They all drove out to South Dakota in a rented motor home. Shawn was helpful watching out for his younger brother Tony. He also assisted with Elaine's elderly parents. Shawn was fun to be around. They enjoyed seeing the buffalo, the Black Hills, Mount Rushmore, Crazy Horse Memorial and Devil's Tower in South Dakota.

(L to R) Lucille, Elaine, Shawn, Tony and Bob at Devil's Tower, South Dakota, 1996 Summer.

After Shawn got back from his wonderful vacation, he reached another milestone in his young life. Almost every 16-year-old young man wants to have his driver's license and Shawn was no exception. Shawn completed his driver's education requirements, passed his driver's test and earned his probationary driver's license. This was awesome because this confirmed that Shawn was seizure-free.

In October of 1996, I went on a four-day (Thursday-Sunday) Cursillo retreat with several members from my church. The retreat was held in Washburn, WI. During the retreat, a team of religious and lay personnel presented a series of talks to the participants of the retreat. This retreat provided enlightenment in my spiritual walk regarding community and the sacraments. The retreat was located about 3 hours away from my home. Shawn, who was almost 17 years old, wanted to stay home alone. I was very hesitant about allowing Shawn to stay home by himself. Yet he was scheduled to work the entire weekend. Shawn's little brother Tony was staying at his dad's house. My mother was only a couple of blocks away in case of an emergency. For these three reasons, I agreed to let Shawn stay at the house by himself. At this time we had a Chevrolet Caprice classic. It was a BIG car. While I was gone, Shawn had strict orders from me NOT to drive the car. On Friday Shawn decided to take the car and give a couple of his friends a ride to school. When Shawn was backing out of the driveway onto the road, he looked to see if any cars were coming. He was looking eastward and the sun was shining so bright, he could not see anything. He backed out anyway, right underneath the big yellow school bus that he was supposed to be riding. The bus ran over the backend of the car and smashed it up. Luckily, he and his passengers were NOT injured and no one was hurt on the bus! They called my mother and she helped Shawn and his buddies get to school.

On the last day of the retreat the family members and loved ones are invited to attend the closing ceremony. My mom made the trip to participate in this ceremony. After we were all done, and we were so happy and life was good, my mom pulled me aside and shared something incredible with me. She told me the whole story about Shawn driving the car and smashing it up underneath the school bus. I was so relieved that no one was hurt, yet I was livid because Shawn did not do as we had agreed! Someone could have been seriously injured! The consequence for Shawn's disobedience was that now he did not have a car that he could drive.

In September of 1996, Shawn started confirmation class. The class met every Wednesday evening for a full year. In November of 1996 Shawn went on a Teens Encounter Christ (TEC)) retreat for his confirmation class. This was a very special weekend for Shawn. His cousin, Jesse Wulf was there, too. This is how Jesse remembers Shawn: *"My memories of Shawn that I remember most were when we ended up at the same TEC (Teens Encounter Christ) retreat. That was the first time I actually got to know Shawn. We had a fun weekend. I wish I would have gotten the time to go on another one with him and gotten the chance to know him better."*

I know Shawn had a spiritual experience and met Jesus, in a personal way during the retreat. Because his retreat was so close to mine, we were able to share the experiences of our retreats together. We both felt a lot closer to God. We wanted to do better in our personal lives. Shawn was an obedient, respectful and delightful son.

The next big event in Shawn's life was when he was 17. He was confirmed with his cousin, Mike Stock, and the other 13 confirmation candidates at St. Patrick's Catholic Church in Centuria, WI. The confirmation was held on October 19, 1997. After the confirmation ceremony, we had a party at our house to celebrate this blessed event. I was exceedingly thankful to God that I was able to witness my son's transition from a child to an adult in the eyes of our church. Shawn shared that this was one of the most significant events in his life. He was thankful for his newfound faith and his relationship with God, which gave his life meaning and purpose. Here is the Confirmation letter that Shawn wrote in his own words, to the Bishop:

Dear Bishop Raphael Fliss,

You don't how much I look forward to the time when I am confirmed. It's one of those events that are most important in your life like graduation, marriage, and the birth of your children. It has been quite an adventure these past two years. I started out thinking, "I don't need to do all this stuff to be confirmed, I will just lie and say I did everything." But all that changed once I made my first TEC (Teens Encounter Christ). It opened up my eyes making me realize that I needed to do those requirements for myself, to make me a better person, to put others before myself. So after that, I started doing little jobs at first, then going up to bigger and more important jobs. As I did these tasks I started to feel a lot better about myself after looking at a job well done.

Before Confirmation started, I thought I knew a lot about the Bible. I mean, I had one beside my bed and read the whole thing about once a week. But when I was doing the questions, I realized that what I knew wasn't enough. I still had a lot to learn about the bible. So as I was reading my bible, I learned more stuff than I thought existed. I am glad that I had another chance to take a look.

These past two years have been the best so far in my life, with a senior and me almost being confirmed. I am just so anxious to go out into the real-world helping others as I do now. Some people complain that Confirmation isn't the best, but I for one think it's a blast.

Sincerely,

Shawn P. Woolley

At 17 Shawn made his confirmation. Brother Ryan was sponsor. (L to R) Ryan, Father Dan Dahlberg, Shawn, Bishop Fliss.

When Shawn turned 18 in February of 1998, he did not imbibe in adult beverages, even though in the state of Wisconsin, that was legally allowed. He made the responsible choice because he was taking medications for his seizures and his ADD. Shawn dispensed and took his own medication.

Shawn graduated from Osceola High School on May 15, 1998. There were 110 students in his graduating class. Their class motto was: *"What lies behind us and what lies before us are small matters compared to what lies within us"* Ralph Waldo Emerson.

Before his graduation I asked Shawn if he wanted me to invite his biological dad and grandparents to his high school graduation. Shawn said yes, he would like to meet them face-to-face for the first time. We had talked about Shawn's biological dad several times before. We contacted him when we filled out Shawn's family tree. I had previously asked Shawn's biological dad several time if he wanted to see Shawn. He always said no. Now that Shawn was an adult, his biological dad agreed to meet Shawn. His biological dad had regularly paid child support for Shawn's care. I was so happy that Shawn said yes and hoped that this would provide a missing piece to the puzzle in his life. The courage that took for Shawn to say yes was huge. After Shawn's graduation ceremony, he met his biological dad face-to-face for the first time. What an experience! This was the moment that Shawn and I had been awaiting for 18 years! After all this time, there was some tension and awkwardness. They shook hands and hugged each other. Shawn was relieved to meet his biological dad. He was glad that his dad had taken the effort to come to see him graduate from high school. We all took pictures together to remember this special moment. Shawn's biological dad assured Shawn that he would see him again at his graduation party in a few weeks at our home.

Celebrating after Shawn's graduation ceremony.

Several weeks later we had a big party to celebrate Shawn's graduation. Shawn's brothers and sister, Grandma Vera, aunts and uncles, cousins, friends, his stepdad Greg and Elaine, his biological dad and grandparents all came to help us celebrate this big event. After the party, both Shawn's biological dad and grandparents shared that they wanted to stay in touch with Shawn in the future. They welcomed him to contact them whenever he liked. This was a joyous celebration of the completion of his high school education. Shawn was on center stage. It was all about him! Shawn was really enjoying his life. We were all proud of him and he was so happy.

Shawn's graduation picture for the class of '98.

In July of 1998, after high school graduation, Shawn left his job at Hardees. They were sorry to see him go. They understood about him getting ready to go on to get a higher education. This summer was all about Shawn. He went to visit his Uncle Larry in Elizabeth, MN. He stayed there for over a month. Shawn worked at Larry's convenience store. They went fishing a lot! One day, while Shawn and Uncle Larry were out fishing in the boat, a crazy and funny thing happened. Shawn leaned over the edge of the boat, looking for a big fish and his prescription glasses fell off of his head and into the lake. We will never know how big that fish was, and he never found his glasses! When Shawn came home from Uncle Larry's, he told me how much fun he had working and fishing. He really liked all of the fish they had caught, cooked and eaten.

This is how Uncle Larry remembers Shawn: *"I really got to know Shawn when he came up to work at the store. Shawn was a good worker; he liked working in the Deli and doing what needed to be done. Shawn liked the cat and was good with animals. He was a sensitive young man and felt things with his heart. Shawn went out fishing several times with me, and he really enjoyed fishing. We caught a large walleye one day that was about 30 inches long. He always liked TV and movies."*

Shawn went out fishing several times with his Uncle Larry. He really enjoyed fishing. They caught a large walleye one day that was about 30 inches long.

When summer was over and Shawn returned home from Uncle Larry's, he started looking into furthering his education. During the summer of 1998, Shawn and I worked together on getting him ready to attend the school of his choice. Shawn decided he wanted to attend St. Paul Technical Institute in the big city of St. Paul, MN. The program he chose was graphic arts. We got him registered and went to the school orientation for new students. Shawn was hoping to be able to use his creative, artistic skills and get a good job after he completed his technical training. This was his first adventure out into the real world, as an adult.

Shawn was now going on to school in St. Paul, MN. I was working in Eastern Minneapolis, MN. Osceola, WI was well over an hours drive a way. I decided it would be best for us to move closer to the Twin Cities. I found a very nice house, close to our old neighborhood in Hudson, WI and we moved back there in August of 1998.

The technical school was a huge disappointment to Shawn. Shawn was discouraged. He said his instructor was never in the classroom, and he felt he was not learning what he wanted to. Also, Shawn could not use his artistic creative ability in the class because graphic arts is very structured, and the drawings and art had to be done a specific way. I was allowed to see Shawn's grades. He was not doing well. Because of these challenges in January 1999, Shawn quit the St. Paul Technical Institute. I was heartbroken for Shawn. Now what was he going to do?

Soon after Shawn left school, he got a job at Menards (a local lumber store). While at Menards, Shawn became discouraged when he experienced his supervisor bullying him and making fun of him. Shawn soon quit that job. He started realizing that being an adult was not going to be as fun and free as he thought when he was a youngster. That year, these experiences became two big disappointments in his young, adult life that left a lasting impression on Shawn. After being surrounded by adults who loved and cared about him all of his life, these were new, unpleasant experiences for Shawn. As we see, Shawn's way of dealing with hostile adults was to leave the situation rather than to "stay and learn" how to cope with them. As adults, we are all going to meet up with people who are cruel. Things are not always going to go the way we want them to.

(L to R) Tony and kitty, Ryan, Liz (mom) and kitty, Crystal, Shawn and kitty.

On February 12, 2000 we celebrated Shawn's 20th birthday with a family get together at our home! We had a lot of fun talking, eating delicious food and having a wonderful family time!

Shawn took his birthday money and purchased his **FIRST** MMORPG (Massive Multiplayer Online Role-Playing Game) called Everquest This **one** decision radically altered Shawn's life. This was a tragic game changer. How can one video game change a person's life forever? In the chapters ahead, we will find out how that came to pass.

Chapter 3: Reality Leaves and Fantasy Begins!

"It is better to resolve a conflict then to dissolve a relationship."
Leo Buscaglia

Life in the Woolley household drastically changed after Shawn's 20th birthday. A new force, a video game, was now in play in his life. Shawn was living at my home at the time. Next Shawn got a job delivering pizzas at Domino's Pizza in Hudson, WI. His older brother Ryan used to work there. Shawn was prompt, reliable, hardworking and trustworthy. In April, Shawn was promoted to assistant manager at Dominos' pizza. (Great trivia question - How many dots on the Domino pizza box?) He was now a productive adult. I encouraged him to become more independent. We talked about him moving out of the house and getting his own place. Shawn was thankful and appreciative for this opportunity. Within the next couple of months, Shawn found a place and moved out and rented a room in Hudson that was closer to his work. Shawn bought his first car, a brown Monte Carlo. Shawn paid for his own car insurance. He was becoming a contributing adult to society.

(Answer to trivia question...   3).

51

Shawn became heavily involved with the Everquest video game quite quickly. He was on a Player vs. Player server called Vallon Zek (this was a more violent video game than the video games that were on the Player vs. Monster servers.) It did not take long before Shawn started having some negative effects from playing the Everquest video game in his real life.

I would visit Shawn on a weekly basis. I noticed that Shawn was not eating right or getting enough sleep. He was not taking his seizure medication and he was playing the Everquest video game so much that he started having seizures again. It had been 13 years since Shawn had his last seizure. Being on his own, Shawn had less adult supervision. He was now in charge of his own life and seemed to be making some poor choices regarding how he was living his life. Shawn started to become reclusive. He did not visit us, his family or leave his house and socialize with other people outside of work.

Originally I just thought the Everquest video game was just another regular, average, fun computer video game and so did Shawn. This was the farthest thing from the truth. The Everquest MMORPG (Massive Multiplayer Online Role-Playing Game) was not designed just for the entertainment of the human mind. On January 26, 1999, then current president of Verant Interactive Inc. (soon to be President of Sony On-line Entertainment), John Smedley described Verant Interactive in the following way: *"Verant's commitment to the online gaming community is to push Internet gaming to new heights by creating and maintaining highly addictive, immersive and persistent gaming environments"*. See **Appendix C: The Birth of the Everquest Video Game**. This Everquest video game was purposely designed to be as addicting as possible.

Shawn on my computer at my house.

Shawn had been playing computer games for about the past 10 years, with no major character or social changes in his life and he had not been having any seizures. Shawn was a growing, maturing, productive young man. Those video games that he had been playing were designed for fun and entertainment (i.e. solitaire, Pac man, Space Invaders, Donkey Kong, Doom, etc.). Those video games had a beginning AND an end.

Sony On-Line created and distributed the Everquest video game. Everquest was one of the first of the "new generation" of video games specifically designed by people with degrees in psychology hired by Sony to make the video games as addicting as possible. These new video games (MMORPG) have become "virtual societies". There is no beginning or end to the game. Now the video gaming companies systematically release updates to the games with new levels and more content. The gamer cannot leave the game without losing their status in the game. Also, the game is now the place where the gamer's peers are. If they quit the video game, they will no longer have contact with their "friends".

Below is a letter I received from a TV producer in September of 2003. He shares about psychologists being on the Everquest staff.

*"I found your website profoundly interesting specifically because I am in development of a TV show that focuses on the MMORPG phenomenon. I am currently pitching this network on a 6-program episodic show that will focus on specific players. I wondered if you might provide a lead to MMORPG players whose lives have been transformed, destroyed, altered profoundly, etc. through the playing of these games. **Also interesting are the developers. I interviewed some of the people out at EVERQUEST some years ago, I was amazed to find psychologists amongst the staff. I wonder what other techniques are being used to keep players glued to the box.***

Would greatly appreciate a prompt response, I am meeting development people on Thursday."

Jay D.

I was enlightened to get this letter, to prove that the video games were purposely designed by people with degrees in psychology making video games as addicting as possible.

Today, video gaming is big business. The video gaming companies spend tens of millions of dollars a year on "research" to see how they can keep the people addicted to these video games. They have become no better than drug pushers getting their own customers addicted to the video games so they can rely on the steady stream of income an addicted gamer provides.

The weekend before July 4, 2000 was our town's 48th annual celebration called Hudson Booster Days. This is when the town has its fair. Markets, circus rides, parade and bands come to town. Booster Days is one of the major social events in the summer, thus one of the busiest weekends of the year for Hudson, WI. All of the business owners love this weekend. Visitors from all around come to Booster Days.

On July 2, 2000, after a long stint on the computer playing the Everquest video game, Shawn had a grand mal seizure. He was all bruised up physically and wiped-out mentally. Shawn was scheduled to work at Dominos that day. Even after this major physical episode, he went to work at Dominos anyway because he was the assistant manager. Shawn should have called in sick for work and stayed home, yet Shawn believed it was the right thing to do, to go to work. In the evening when things started slowing down at work and it came time to send someone home, Shawn asked the manager if he could leave and go home because he was not feeling well because of the seizure he had earlier in the day. The manager decided to send someone else home instead. Shawn was devastated by the manager's decision. Shawn decided to walk out, and quit his job that night because he was physically incapable of finishing the shift. Shawn really struggled with feeling that he had been taken advantage of and taken for granted.

This was another example in Shawn's adult life, where Shawn "left" the situation rather than seeking a better way to resolve it. Some of Shawn's choices were made because of his lack of experience as a young adult. He was adept at avoiding conflict in his life rather than confronting it. That was his nature. In high school, Shawn was not into competitive sports. Participating in sports involves constant challenges and decision-making in a fast-paced environment. Shawn was not comfortable in those situations. He was creative and had a gentle soul; he preferred the arts and music. Experience in life gives us wisdom. As a young adult, Shawn still had a LOT to learn about life and people, as we all do. As we experience life and various situations, we can observe the outcomes of our reactions and decisions. We can choose to grow and learn from them. We can gain wisdom that helps us recognize better alternatives in dealing with problems when they arise. We can turn mistakes or failures into learning experiences and make better choices, **next time**. We all experience failures and mistakes in our lives! It is how we choose to respond to them that counts. Here is a link to an inspirational story about **If Only ... Next Time**:

https://www.olganon.org/forum/readings-recovery/if-only-next-time

Shawn went back to the place where he lived and stayed there from July to September. Shawn was changing. He was becoming someone I did not know. He became withdrawn and depressed and anti-social. He stopped shaving and taking care of himself. Shawn had no contact with anyone other than his landlord and me. When I went to see Shawn from July to September, he made me fully aware that he did not appreciate my visits. Shawn was not friendly towards me and was not happy to see me. He did not greet me with a hello or a hug. He would demand gruffly, "What do you want? What are you doing here?" After Shawn quit his job at Dominos, I tried to get him to come home to live and he refused. I worried about Shawn and his health and well-being. As reported by his landlord, Shawn was playing the Everquest game, day and night. He did not get another job. The landlord told me that Shawn was stealing his food and not paying his rent. Shawn could no longer afford his car. He couldn't pay for gas or his insurance.

July 2000 Shawn, after playing Everquest for 6 months.

As a result of all of that, in September of 2000, Shawn was evicted from the house, as he had not paid the rent since July. I would not let Shawn move back into my house unless he agreed to seek professional help. Shawn agreed to this requirement. This was my version of tough love.

With this new understanding, Shawn came back to my house to live. I contacted a therapist in Hudson for Shawn to see so he could get some help for his video gaming problem. After several sessions the therapist informed me "You should be glad Shawn is not addicted to drugs or alcohol." The therapist did not consider Shawn's excessive video gaming to be a problem. I thought, how could this not be a problem? My son, Shawn, just lost his job, apartment, health and car because he was playing video games. The therapist said this to me, right in front of Shawn. It was clear that the therapist did not see his playing video games as a major problem. This gave Shawn the green light to continue with his excessive video gaming playing. Shawn looked directly at me and said, "This is your problem, mom, not mine." Now Shawn's addiction was my problem. In Shawn's mind, there was nothing wrong with him playing this Everquest video game all of the time.

Shawn and I started having disagreements about his life. Shawn was escaping into the Everquest video game so he did not have to go out into the ugly, 'real' adult world. In the game Shawn had no responsibility and if he came up against bullies or unpleasantness, he could just leave it. All he did was play the Everquest video game. Shawn did not get a job or go back to school. He stopped thinking about his future and goals. Shawn told me I should support him so he could play the Everquest video game the rest of his life. Shawn was also stealing my credit cards and charging his video gaming expenses to them. I called the credit card companies to block those charges, as they were unauthorized. I also had to start hiding my purse and credit cards, so Shawn could not find them. I became frustrated and exhausted from all of the drama Shawn and that Everquest video game were creating in my life. I knew something had to change. This craziness could not continue.

Shawn was addicted to this video game. I could not believe it. I was in Alcoholics Anonymous (A.A.) for many years. I was aware of how addicts behaved. I was prepared to take specific steps if any of my children ever got addicted to drugs or alcohol. I knew where I was going to send them, and what I was going to do to get them help. Never did I think my child would get addicted to a video game! There was nowhere to go for help! I had **NEVER** heard of anyone becoming addicted to playing a video game before! This craziness and on-going drama lasted for several months.

On December 22, 2000 I made Shawn leave my house. I could not do this anymore! I was worried that my supporting him was enabling him to stay stuck in his addiction. The day I made him leave, I was so disheartened, I did not know what else to do. I felt like I was going insane. It was either him or me. I had to get him out of my house for my own sanity. In my recovery, we were taught that if someone did not want to take care of themselves we were not supposed to do it for him or her. That is called tough love. I took Shawn to a local motel and helped him get situated. He had enough money to stay there for at least a week. Shawn was happy to leave. He thought he was going on a vacation. He got to stay in a motel by himself and watch all of the TV shows he wanted, when he wanted. He had enough money for some food. He was a happy camper! The only thing Shawn was missing out of his new "happy" life was a computer and the Everquest game.

I now know that kicking an addicted video gamer out of the house is not a good idea because it further isolates them, especially 3 days before Christmas. It was my hope that by doing this, it would be a wake-up call for Shawn. He would be away from my computer, get a job and get himself plugged back into the real adult world. I know now that one of the withdrawal symptoms of removing a game from a gaming addict can be extreme anger. Recent news stories tell of video gaming addicts committing suicide, killing their parents and killing their siblings when the video games were suddenly removed or when they were not allowed to play the video games. Some video gaming addicts are mentally incapable of taking care of themselves because the video gaming disengages their brain. Recovery for a video gaming addict requires on-going treatment and/or lots of contact with people so they can learn to be human beings again rather than just zombies plucking at a keyboard or video game controller. Their brains need to re-wire and get healthy (could take from 30 days to several years). They need to learn/re-learn self-care before they can re-enter the real world. Even today there are very few support meetings for addicted video gamers because the recovering gamers are not capable of starting and leading meetings to help themselves and others. They cannot even personally take care of themselves. I could see this clearly, in my own son, Shawn. He needed help NOW!

Chapter 4: Thanks for a Miracle!

"When we do the best we can, we never know what miracle is wrought in our life, or in the life of another." Helen Keller

I was able to get Shawn help from the county social services, thanks to a miracle. On December 23, 2000, less then 24 hours after I moved Shawn out of my house, I was having problems with my water filter in the kitchen. I called a local plumbing company several times to come out and fix it. They never called back. Then I called a plumbing company in Roberts, WI, a neighboring town. The company said their plumber could come out the next day, which was Christmas Eve. I was ecstatic to know that a plumber would come out to my house on Christmas Eve to fix my plumbing! What an early Christmas gift! This was my miracle in this season of miracles!

The plumber came out the next day around noon. He was working on replacing the water filter. We were having a conversation. I asked him what he was getting his wife for Christmas. He proceeded to tell me he was getting her a beautiful ring. I said she must be really special to deserve that. He said she is very special. I asked him what she did. He answered that she worked for a program in the neighboring county. I asked him what kind of program. He said it was a program that helped people of all ages, who have long-term problems, to live independently. My ears perked up.

My heart started to race. I asked him if that program was available in St. Croix County, where we lived. He said it was set up to work in three counties. St. Croix County was included. I was so excited I was beside myself. This is what Shawn needed. Right then, while he was standing there, I got his wife's phone number and called her. I told her about the situation with my son. She said that if Shawn qualified, he could be a candidate for this program. She then told me who to contact in my county to get him enrolled. This really lightened my burden because I now knew there was hope for my son.

Shawn and I spent Christmas Eve at his stepdad Greg and Elaine's house with his little brother Tony. Because we were able to get the plumbing fixed and had a promising plan for Shawn's future, we enjoyed the Christmas Eve celebration together. The boys got some wonderful gifts. The next day we all went to Christmas mass at St. Patrick's church in Hudson, WI. What a beautiful place and time to thank God for all of his wonderful grace and mercy in our family's life. We then went home and ate a delicious Christmas dinner and had a nice, relaxing Christmas evening.

2000 Christmas. Shawn and I spent Christmas Eve at his stepdad's with his little brother, Tony. (L to R) Tony, Liz, Shawn.

SHAWN'S DIAGNOSIS

On Tuesday, the day after Christmas, I called the county for information about the long-term support program to see if Shawn was eligible. The county called me back on Wednesday. We made an appointment to see Dr. John Ei, a psychiatrist with the county for an evaluation of Shawn in January 2001. This evaluation included thorough mental testing to see if Shawn qualified for the long-term support program. In the meantime the county did a temporary emergency placement of Shawn into a group home. We moved Shawn from the motel to the group home. I was very grateful for the county and this new residential program. I was also appreciative of their providing the services and testing for Shawn.

In February, we received Shawn's diagnosis from Dr. Ei. This is the transcript of the diagnosis:

Shawn is a 20-year-old man with average intelligence who appears capable of post high school work, if he is more motivated and can compensate for emotional problems. He appears to be struggling with major depression, Dysthymia and passive dependency schizoid personality characteristics. He is currently living in a group home because he cannot keep a job himself.

DSM IV DIAGNOSIS:
Axis I: Major Depression; Dysthymia; Social Anxiety; and Avoidant Behavior
Axis II: Passive Dependent and Schizoid Personality and Characteristics.
Axis III: History of Seizure Disorder
Axis IV: Moderate Stress from Social Anxiety and a feeling that he cannot do anything.
Axis V: GAF 30-40

Shawn had been playing the Everquest game for a year. Playing that video game was the start of a downhill spiral in my son's life. At this time, no medical person I knew had ever heard of or recognized "video gaming as an addiction". That is why it is not listed in Shawn's diagnosis. As a result of this diagnosis, Shawn was accepted into the long-term support program.

I think it is important that I share with you the definition of a Schizoid Personality Disorder* per the Mayo Clinic, so you don't confuse it with the definition of Schizophrenia:

> *"Schizoid personality disorder is an uncommon condition in which people avoid social activities and consistently shy away from interaction with others. It affects more males than females. If you have schizoid personality disorder, you may be seen as a loner, and you may lack the desire or skill to form close personal relationships.*
>
> *To others, you may appear somewhat dull or humorless. Because you don't tend to show emotion, you may appear as though you don't care about what's going on around you. Although you may seem aloof, you may actually feel lonely, even if it's hard for you to acknowledge. Or you may feel much more at ease being alone, and feel comfortable with your life. "*

The above description of a Schizoid personality described Shawn at this time. He was not a schizophrenic. He was such a changed person, from before he started playing that addicting Everquest video game.

*Here is the link to the full schizoid disorder definition: http://www.mayoclinic.org/diseases-conditions/schizoid-personality-disorder/basics/definition/CON-20029184
OR To read the entire definition, do a search on the internet for: Mayo Clinic and Schizoid Personality Disorder.

Before Shawn started playing the Everquest video game, he was sensitive, shy, happy and a smart young man. He had a gentle spirit and was a sweet, caring and loving person. He had a sense of humor and he was goofy, especially if there was a camera focused on him! He seemed vulnerable. He had a keen sense of observing the world around him and at the same time, not really able to make sense of it all. Shawn was not a tough or competitive person because he wanted people to like him. He was adventurous. Shawn was not afraid of anything. He could be talked into doing almost anything.

After one year of Shawn's growing addiction to the Everquest video game, this MMORPG video game was a major factor in the negative change of Shawn's life and character. Before his twentieth birthday, he was a kind, creative, friendly, funny, hardworking, and sensitive young man. One year later, after his twenty-first birthday, Shawn was diagnosed as a dull, humorless, lonely, depressed person. It almost seemed like Shawn was a shell of the human being he used to be. I am so angry and disgusted that today, many years later, there still is no approved diagnosis for video gaming addiction or disorder in the DSM (Diagnostic Statistical Manual of Mental Disorders).

GETTING HELP FOR SHAWN

The county got back to us, and Shawn was accepted into the program called Long Term Support. I was relieved and happy that Shawn was accepted into this program. Immediately Shawn was placed in a group home in North Hudson with a couple of other young men. The doctors and psychiatrist prescribed this for Shawn's new medication regiment: his Cylert medication was removed and Serzone, 150 mgs. 2 q H S was prescribed for depression, as was Effexor XR 75 mgs 2 q a.m. for depression. There was supervision at the group home to make sure Shawn took his medication. Also, the staff took him to his appointments with his doctor, psychiatrist and therapist. This living arrangement worked well for Shawn. There was no computer in the group home, and Shawn had "some" socialization with real people and adult supervision.

Shawn started doing better. He started coming out of his shell and was more interactive with us, his family. Shawn was smiling more and he was friendlier. Shawn was nicer and kinder to me. His personal hygiene was also improving. I was so relieved and hopeful. However, the game still had a firm hold over him.

If Shawn wanted to play the Everquest game, he had to walk to our house. We lived about 5 miles from the group home where he was staying. Despite the distance, he still made the trek. A lot of times, he came over when I was at work or I was sleeping at night. Nobody really knew how much Shawn was playing the Everquest game. For example, one night, about 2:00 A.M., I woke up and couldn't sleep. This is unusual for me, because I don't have a problem sleeping. It was like my spirit was restless. Rather than just lie there, I decided to get up and check my email. The computer was across the house, in the guest room. I was sitting there, reading my emails, when I heard my front door open. I freaked out! Who would be coming into my house at this time of the morning? I was looking for a baseball bat to hit the intruder over the head! I almost fainted in terror, wondering who on earth it could be! I quietly snuck down the hallway and peeked around the corner to see who it was. There stood Shawn! I asked him "What on earth are you doing here, at 2 in the morning?" He casually said he was just coming over, to check his email. Right! He was coming over to play that video game! I wondered to myself, how long Shawn had been feeding his addiction at 2 o'clock in the morning at my house?

A couple of days later I had a conversation with Shawn's little brother Tony, who was 13 years old. Tony shared with me that more than once Shawn was at the house playing the video game when he went to bed. When Tony got up to go to school in the morning, Shawn was still at the house, playing the Everquest game.

With this new information, I immediately contacted the long-term support group staff and told them I needed to meet with them, to inform them of what I had found out. They said they would not meet with me, because I was not Shawn's legal guardian. I was able to meet with Shawn's psychiatrist, Dr. Ei, and asked him for his solution to getting Shawn off of the Everquest game. Dr. Ei said that he had talked with Shawn about his excessive gaming. Shawn said that was the only thing he liked to do. Dr. Ei agreed with Shawn that he could keep playing the Everquest game. To me, this was utterly ridiculous. It was like telling an alcoholic, that if drinking is the only thing you like to do, keep drinking! Or telling a drug addict that if heroin is all you like to do, keep doing it. I was really disappointed that, again, the mental health community did not recognize Shawn's excessive gaming as a problematic behavior that was contributing to his addiction. The "professionals" did not treat this activity/behavior as an addiction. Yet the results were the same, for my son. In April of 2001, Shawn had another grand mal seizure. He had been playing the Everquest video game for hours on end.

Did you know that the flickering lights in video games can trigger seizures in someone who is seizure prone and plays video games too long? That is called photosensitive epilepsy*. The following is the definition as defined by WebMD:

> People with photosensitive _epilepsy_ have seizures that are triggered by:
> - Flashing lights
> - Bold, contrasting visual patterns (such as stripes or checks)
> - Overexposure to video games
>   Anti-epileptic medicines are available to reduce the risk of a seizure. But people with photosensitive epilepsy should take steps to minimize their exposure to seizure triggers.

There was no controlling the time Shawn spent on the game. I took the computer keyboard to work with me, so he could not play. I later found out he had bought another keyboard without my knowledge. I found it hidden in the closet. I explained to Shawn to please stop playing the video game because that is causing him to have these seizures. Shawn was so addicted to the game, that he did not care if he had seizures or not. Shawn had never seen anyone have a grand mal seizure. Personally seeing someone have a grand mal seizure is a VERY terrifying experience!

*The following link is to the full article that describes the photosensitive epileptic medical condition:
https://www.webmd.com/epilepsy/guide/photosensitive-epilepsy-symptoms-causes-treatment#1

In May 2001 Shawn was living and doing okay at the group home. He was now well enough to get a new job at Papa Murphy's Pizza in Hudson, WI. This was a new business in our town. I was excited for Shawn as he started this new phase in his life. Shawn was glad to be working again, making money and meeting new people.

Shawn decided he wanted his own apartment. He spoke to his therapist and the Long-Term Support team about getting his own place. They said they would help him get an apartment. Both his stepfather, Greg and I requested they NOT get Shawn an apartment, because he needed the adult supervision and assistance he was getting in the group home. Because Shawn was 21 years old, and I was not his legal guardian, they would not listen to Greg or me. They said he was not a danger to himself, or to others. If that is what Shawn wanted, they would help him get a place of his own. This was the start of what turned my Christmas miracle of a group home into the nightmare of him getting his own place.

Chapter 5: From a Miracle to a Nightmare

"When baseball is no longer fun, it is no longer a game."
Joe DiMaggio

With the help of the people at the long-term support program, Shawn found an apartment in Hudson, WI, and signed a lease. Shawn moved into his new apartment at the beginning of June of 2001. The apartment number was 104. At this time, Shawn did not have a car. The apartment was located within walking distance of his job, the grocery store and a shopping center. It was an adequate place for him. Over the next couple of weeks, as we found pieces of furniture, we moved them into his apartment. It was furnished nicely. Shawn also took two of our cats, named George and Butternut, to his apartment in Hudson. He loved his kitties.

Shawn (R) and his little brother Tony (L), in his new apartment.

After Shawn was settled in, his younger brother, Tony and I went to visit him. I hinted that now that he had this nice place, he could invite us over for a meal once in a while. Shawn was a good cook! I thought his response was rather odd. Shawn said we could come over the weekend before Thanksgiving, and he would cook us up a nice meal. I was disappointed. It was June. I wondered why Shawn wanted to wait that long, and why on that particular day? I said, "Well, okay".

Shawn did not have a computer at his new apartment. He had purchased his own video gaming system. Shawn still had to come to our house to play his Everquest computer game. His new apartment was closer to my house than the group home was. It was only 1.8 miles away. We as a family, were still trying to control how much he was playing that video game.

My oldest son Ryan, and his fiancée moved into my home in preparation for their wedding in July. We as a family all agreed to attempt to limit Shawn's time on the computer, to one hour a day, so he wouldn't have more seizures. It didn't work. Soon Shawn started playing the Everquest video game a lot again!

Shawn did not talk to us or his other friends very much anymore. He quit going on outings with his little brother, Tony. They used to play golf together and shoot hoops. They were the best of buds. Shawn said his "real" friends were in the Everquest game now and that he only trusted them. This saddened me greatly. I tried to explain to Shawn that the characters were only pixels and not real people. He did not care. To Shawn the characters in the Everquest video game were "real"!

As a mother I saw that Shawn was withdrawing more and more into himself. He was losing those sensitive, caring, loving human traits he once had. He was withdrawing and becoming cold, distant, numb and anti-social, shutting out his family, even his little brother, Tony.

FIRST BETRAYAL TO SHAWN IN THE GAME

The culture of the gamer world can be very cruel. For some gamers, the video games become more than just a video game. A person can get sucked into these virtual worlds, and this becomes their new reality. The gamer may start to treat other characters in the games as real people. In June of 2001 Shawn's first big "betrayal" by someone in the Everquest game took place. Shawn was not in a guild in the Everquest game. (A guild is a medieval group of merchants or craftsmen with similar association.) Shawn and another person hung out together in the game and helped each other out. When one was not on the game they would hold the other person's "loot" because they did not trust the "banks" in the game. Shawn and this other person had been friends for many months in the game. One day Shawn went back in the game to play and his "friend" who had meant so much to him had stolen all of Shawn's loot and disappeared. Shawn was devastated. Later, Shawn confided in me about what happened in the game. He almost started crying. He wasn't angry. He was so hurt that this new "friend", who he had put so much trust in for so long, would betray him. He stole all of Shawn's money, treasures and disappeared. Shawn never heard from him again! It is hard to comprehend that Shawn, who chose not trust his mom or his family and his real friends, would put all of his faith into someone he never met, in a video game!

I thought Shawn was going to quit the Everquest game and encouraged him to do that. Shawn actually stopped playing Everquest for several weeks because he was so devastated that his friend in the video game violated his trust so completely. I thought we had Shawn back in his real life. However, Shawn was soon back playing the Everquest game again.

By now Shawn's real life was flat-lining. There was nothing left there except his job at Papa Murphy's. He needed his job so he could earn money to pay his rent. This is where the addiction took over. This is where the demons claimed his mind again. This is where, if he had proper addiction therapy and supervision, he might still be alive today. No matter how bad it got in the game, he still wanted to play because he had nowhere else that he wanted to be. I now see that this was a pivotal point in Shawn's life. The choices in his gaming addiction were really affecting his life. Shawn was either going to get delivered from the game now, or be pulled back into that cesspool of deviancy – video gaming addiction.

The next big event in Shawn's life was when his older brother, Ryan, got married on July 14, 2001. This was a joyous, family occasion. Shawn came to the wedding and participated in the family pictures before the ceremony. After the ceremony, I looked for Shawn at the church and could not find him. At the reception, everyone was asking about Shawn because they missed him and his humor and playful antics. He was a fun-loving guy and liked goofing-off with others, especially at family events. When I went home after the reception and dance, Shawn was sitting there at my house, playing the Everquest game. Later, I discovered that after the family pictures Shawn had walked back to my house, without my knowledge and without my blessing. This was not like Shawn. He used to love parties and enjoyed participating in family events. This was another example of Shawn living out his addiction in his fantasy world of the Everquest game, and ignoring his family, his friends and his real life.

(L to R) Shawn, Liz, Ryan, Crystal, Tony at big brother Ryan's wedding.

There were many times when I tried to communicate with Shawn about his life. Sadly, Everquest had much more influence over Shawn than I was able to. We were in a long battle. Shawn wanted to play the Everquest game and I wanted him to stop playing. I don't know how many times I deleted that Everquest game off my computer. Soon the game would be right back on my computer. Later in July, because he was playing the Everquest computer game so much, Shawn had several more grand mal seizures. He was NOT playing the Everquest game when I was at the house. He knew I would not have allowed it. When he had these grand mal seizures, Shawn would trash the room he was in. He would knock the dresser over and the painting off of the wall. Sometimes he would cut himself and we found blood splattered all over. Shawn scared the heck out of us, because the seizures were so strong, and he was such a big person. Shawn was over 6 feet tall and weighed over 250 lbs.

A week later, on Friday July 20, Shawn came over to my house to get his "fix" of the Everquest game. I was sound asleep. At 12:30 AM, Shawn had another grand mal seizure while playing the video game. Shawn was stumbling down the basement steps at my home, where his older brother Ryan and his pregnant wife were living. There was such a commotion going on that I woke up from the noise. Ryan stopped Shawn and asked him what he was doing. Shawn was acting out a delusion. He said he thought he was walking in the forest in the Everquest game. This is known as "Game Transfer Phenomenon"* (GTP) and has been extensively studied by Dr. Mark Griffith and Dr. Angelica de Gortari in England.

While having the seizure, Shawn fell off of the chair and got a cut above his eye. This was the incident I believed I needed to get him more professional help. Ryan and I could not get Shawn in the car. He was too big, and he couldn't walk so I called the ambulance. The police came over, too. I had the ambulance take him to the Hudson hospital. Shawn did not know why I called for the ambulance this time. Shawn had had seizures several times before and I had not called for an ambulance. I had a reason. I wanted to see if we could get Shawn committed so we could get him more help for his video game addiction. When we were in the emergency room, I talked with the doctor about Shawn's addiction to the Everquest game. I asked him about committing Shawn to a psychiatric facility to get him help.

*Go to this article for more information about the Game Transfer Phenomenon (GTP):
https://www.vice.com/sv/article/5gqb5d/how-screen-addiction-is-ruining-the-brains-of-children

The doctor's response was minimal. He said we could not do anything unless Shawn threatened to hurt himself or someone else. I believed Shawn's seizure disorder was a threat to himself. I requested that the doctor document that playing the games too much promotes seizures, if the person is seizure prone. On Shawn's discharge papers, the doctor wrote, "Shawn should NOT play the computer game so much". This is the first time that I had documented medical proof that Shawn was playing this Everquest game too much.

I told Shawn that from now on when he had a seizure I was calling the ambulance. I informed Shawn that he would have to pay the bill because I was tired of him not caring enough about himself to stop playing the Everquest game. Shawn was angry with me for calling the ambulance, because now he was going to have to pay that ambulance bill. People with addictions often blame others even when others are trying to help them. They do not want to admit they have a problem. If they did, they will have to do something about it. They will need to give up their "drug of choice", which their brain desperately wants, to "keep feeling good".

After that Shawn's older brother Ryan, his wife and I were extremely upset and totally banned Shawn from ever playing the Everquest game in our home again. Shawn got very angry with his older brother and his wife for doing this. Shawn was already irate with me, because I kept trying to get him to quit playing that Everquest game. He did not care about himself or us, his family, at all. Shawn was obsessed with playing the Everquest game. That was his all-consuming addiction.

Soon after this incident, I had a serious talk with Shawn and asked him if he had ever thought of hurting himself. Shawn said no, he never thought about   anything like that.

In the middle of August I received a call from Shawn. He wanted to know if I could do him a favor. This was a rarity. He seldom called me for anything. I was pleased that he had reached out to me, and was very interested to know what I could do for him. Shawn told me that he saved up his money from work and that he had purchased a used computer from the neighboring town of Amery. Would I be able to give him ride over there, so he could pick it up. He said he needed it so he could get Microsoft certified, and get a job with computers. I was happy to do that. I also thought it would be a good way to have some mother-son time together. I had not seen him much, since he moved into his apartment. We went and got the computer. He set it up in his apartment. To this day, I have nagging guilt about doing that. Today, I believe that I helped him continue his addiction. This was taking a bad situation and making it worst.

Shawn should have been happy now. He had a good job at Papa Murphy's, he had his own apartment, and now, his own computer.

A world-changing event occurred on September 11, 2001. Two hijacked planes crashed into the World Trade Centers in New York City. Another plane was hijacked and crashed into the Pentagon in Washington D.C. A fourth plane that was targeted for the White House was hijacked and drove into the ground in Shanksville, Pennsylvania. Almost 3,000 people died. This affected millions of people around the world, making it a more fearful place in which to live and function. This catastrophe changed people's attitudes, and their secure feelings of safety in their home. My first grandson was supposed to be born on that day. Fortunately he came into the world 10 days later!

With all of this devastation and confusion going on in the world, a bright spot in our lives was the birth of my first grandson, Zachariah. This was Shawn's first nephew. Over a month later, at the end of October, Shawn finally saw his new nephew Zachariah.

Shawn's new nephew Zachariah.

The people Shawn worked with shared with me later, that Shawn talked like he saw Zachariah frequently. This shows more of Shawn's isolation towards family while still pretending that everything was copacetic.

In October, Shawn was either working at Papa Murphy's or at his apartment playing that Everquest game. Shawn had disconnected his phone because he did want to be bothered by the outside world. We could not call and talk with Shawn. We did all of our communication with Shawn at his work place. We called him there and picked him up there if he needed a ride to go shopping or to go to the doctor.

Shawn quit cleaning his apartment. He wouldn't let anyone in to see him. His sister, Crystal, was out of the country for several months. When Crystal got home Shawn was the first person she went to see. Shawn did not answer the door for her. Crystal was heartbroken because Shawn would not let her in so she could visit with him.

Shawn stopped going to his doctor appointments. (I did not find that out, until November.) He had not come over to my house for several months. On Halloween, I went and got Shawn, so he could come over to the house to celebrate and get some candy and pass it out to the trick-or-treaters. We talked a little bit and tried to get caught up with each other's lives. Shawn said he had to tell me something. I did not know what he was going to say. Shawn was having a real hard time telling me. He started to tell me several times, and then he stopped. Finally, after about 20 minutes Shawn told me that he had stopped taking his medications.

I was shocked. I was dumbfounded. "Why???" I asked him. He answered, "Because".

After Shawn told me that he stopped taking his medication, I contacted his caseworker the next day, November 1, to find out what was going on. She said she had not been to his place since August (after Shawn bought his computer). Who knows how many grand mal seizures Shawn had had, all by himself! Shawn would not return his caseworker's phone calls, or let her into his apartment. The only way she could see Shawn, was to call him at his work and go and talk to him on the sidewalk there, for a couple of minutes. The caseworker also informed me, that he had not been to any of his doctor appointments since August. She said they could not tell me this information before for patient privacy reasons because I was not Shawn's legal guardian. I was very concerned. The caseworker said she would contact Shawn and make an appointment to see him. Shawn's caseworker called me and shared with me that she had set up an appointment with Shawn right after Thanksgiving.

A week later Shawn went to an NBA Minnesota Timberwolves basketball game with his younger brother, Tony, and stepdad, Greg. Tony shared with me that he had a great time with his older brother.

On November 11 my family was invited to my mom's house, for our annual "harvest" meal. This was an important tradition in our family that had been going on for over 15 years. Once a year, my family was invited to my mom's house for a meal. Shawn refused to attend. He said he should be able to spend time with his own "friends". I knew he was going to be on that Everquest game because he had stopped contact with his real friends months ago. I was very upset with Shawn because once again, he was putting the Everquest video game before his real family. Shawn stayed in his apartment and played his Everquest game all day long. It was like we did not matter to Shawn at all anymore.

Are there people in your life who matter to you and they don't know it? Take the time to share with them today, what a blessing they are in your life.

Chapter 6: The Final Battle

"The bravest thing I ever did was continuing my life when I
wanted to die... I have the power to say,
This is not how my story will end!" Anonymous

The final battle to get my son back started the week before Thanksgiving. Our family was invited to my sister, Maureen's, for the Thanksgiving Day meal. I was attempting to set up a time with Shawn as to when I would pick him up so we could ride together.

I called Shawn's place of employment, Papa Murphy's on Tuesday, November 12. That is the only place I could get a hold of him. I could not call his home because he had his phone disconnected. Papa Murphy's told me that Shawn was not there. It was his time off. The next day I called again (Wednesday, November 13). They informed me that he did not come in to work. On Thursday evening, the week before Thanksgiving, I finally spoke to the owner, Shawn's boss, Rick Murphy. Rick informed me that Shawn did not come in to work all week. He did not call in to let Rick know that he was not coming in to work. He was concerned about Shawn and was wondering if he was okay. Rick did not know why Shawn did not come in to work. He was not like that. Shawn was very dependable and always came to work when he was scheduled. Or if he was sick, Shawn would call in to notify someone.

The next day, Friday, November 16, I drove over to Shawn's apartment to make sure he was okay. I had not been to his apartment since the middle of August, as he would not answer his door.

I buzzed Shawn at the front security door of his apartment building. Because Shawn had disconnected his phone, I knew he did not know I was there. I had another resident let me into the apartment building. I went to his door and knocked. When Shawn did not answer the door, I called the landlord of the apartment complex to let me into his apartment. The landlord was ill, so her assistant drove to the complex and unlocked the door. There was a security chain on the door, so I could not just walk in. When Shawn heard the door open he got up and came to the door. The assistant left. Shawn said he had been sleeping and had not heard me knock.

Shawn would not let me come into his apartment. He said it was a mess, and he was embarrassed. I peeked around him. I could see that his apartment was cluttered. It looked like a pigsty. I don't think he had cleaned his apartment since he got his computer in August. I did not want to belittle or nag Shawn about cleaning his apartment. I offered to help him clean it up. He declined my help. Shawn said he would clean his apartment by himself. I accepted what he said.

While standing at his chained door, Shawn apologized to me for not cooking the meal he had promised for Tony and me in June. Shawn said his place was too dirty. I had forgotten about the offer of Shawn cooking us a meal. I thanked him and accepted his apology. I was surprised and shocked that he had remembered it.

I asked him why he was not going to work at Papa Murphy's. Shawn informed me that he had quit his job at Papa Murphy's and gotten a new job at Wal-Mart, working the night shift as a shelf stocker. I asked him why he did not inform the owner, who was also his boss that he was quitting. He said, "It doesn't matter, anyway." Those words would come back to haunt me.

I was very disappointed that Shawn had not informed his boss, Rick Murphy of his decision to get a new job. I had my cell phone with me. I told Shawn to call Papa Murphy's and inform his boss that he would no longer be employed there. I handed my cell phone to Shawn through the small opening of the chained door so he could make that call, immediately. I know his boss was upset. Shawn was a very good employee, and for him to leave, with no notice, was not right. Shawn told his boss the same thing that he had told me. It was because he had gotten a different job.

After Shawn was finished talking to his boss, I asked him about Thanksgiving Day. I wanted to figure out what time to pick him up next Thursday. I could not buzz him at his apartment to notify him that I was there. I could not call him because he did not have a phone. Shawn said to talk to him at his new job on Sunday night. He was working the third shift. I was also working the third shift at my job. I would stop there on my way to work early Monday morning and talk with Shawn. There was no contact between us over the weekend.

As per Shawn's instructions, on my way to work early Monday morning, I stopped by Wal-Mart in Hudson, WI. I went to the information desk to ask where I could find Shawn Woolley. They told me they did not have a Shawn Woolley employed there. I said perhaps they were mistaken. Maybe Shawn was too new and they did not know about him yet. I left and went to work. On Tuesday morning, after I finished at my work, I stopped in at Shawn's "new place of employment" again to talk to the day store manager. They would know if Shawn really worked there. The store manager confirmed what the night manager had said. There was no Shawn Woolley employed there. I was disgusted with Shawn. What was Shawn doing now? Why would Shawn quit a job he loved and tell me he was working somewhere else when he really wasn't? I knew I would have to go back to Shawn's apartment and ask him what was going on. I just did not want to deal with it then. Shawn was an adult. I would not nag him. I treated him with the dignity and respect I would show any other adult and let him make his own decisions.

On Wednesday morning, November 21, after work, I went to Shawn's apartment again. I still needed to set up a time to pick him up tomorrow for Thanksgiving dinner. I went into the building when someone else was going in and knocked at his apartment door. Shawn did not answer.

I called the landlord again. She came and unlocked the door to Shawn's apartment. This time Shawn did not come to the door. The chain was still on the door. The landlord told me I should cut it off because it was not supposed to be there because of the fire code. She informed me that she was out of town the next day (Thanksgiving) so she could not let me in then. I would be on my own. She left. I continued to knock at Shawn's door. I looked in as far as I could see (which wasn't very far). I did not see anything. I did not smell anything. I then went outside Shawn's apartment to his windows and pounded on them. I thought if Shawn were sleeping I would attempt to wake him up. Shawn did not come to the window. I chose NOT to break in then. I wanted to leave Shawn his dignity. I knew that tomorrow Shawn would have to answer the door because it was Thanksgiving, and we were going to my sister, Maureen's home for Thanksgiving dinner. I left and went home.

I had to work Thanksgiving morning from 2 AM to 9 AM. After work I drove to Hudson, WI. to pick Shawn up at his apartment. Then we were going to pick up his sister, Crystal. We were all three going to drive to my sister, Maureen's for Thanksgiving to eat dinner together. I was all excited about picking up Shawn and Crystal and going to my sister's. Everybody loved Maureen and her family. I was really looking forward to some quality family time and delicious food.

When I arrived at Shawn's apartment he did not answer his door again. I was getting agitated and upset. I would have to find someone to unlock his apartment door again. Before I went to find someone, I turned the doorknob and realized the door was still unlocked from yesterday. I stopped. Now I was getting scared. Why was the door still unlocked? I opened the door. The security chain was still on the door. I was searching for answers. I needed a clue. What had happened to my son? I could smell something in Shawn's apartment.

There I stood, a single parent, alone, in the hallway, on Thanksgiving morning, in front of my son's apartment door. I was guessing that Shawn was behind it, probably dead. I needed to know what was behind that door. I knew that if I called the police, that they would not let me see my son. I decided to drive home to get a pliers and a crow bar to break into Shawn's apartment as per the landlord's instructions the day before. Terrified, I made that dreadful trip (even though it was less then two miles, it seemed to take forever) to my home staying as calm as I could, trying not to emotionally explode. I got back to the apartment building with the tools and broke the chain off of the door. I walked into Shawn's apartment. Shawn's door to his bedroom was open.

I saw my son, Shawn, in his bedroom. He was sitting on his rocking chair in front of his computer. There was a .22 rifle propped up by his side.

I walked into Shawn's bedroom and glanced around. The computer was still on and the Everquest game was on the computer screen. I saw Shawn, sitting in front of that damn Everquest game. When I looked at Shawn sitting in his chair, I did not know if he was dead or alive. All I saw was him and the gun. I did not touch him. At that time there had been incidents in the news of children killing their parents. I thought maybe he was going to shoot me, and then himself, so I ran out of his apartment.

I called the caretakers of the apartment. The caretaker's husband used to be an Emergency Medical Technician. He came over and went into Shawn's apartment to check on him. He came out into the hallway and told me Shawn was dead. I collapsed in the hallway.

The caretaker then called the Hudson police. The police arrived at Shawn's apartment about 10-15 minutes later. I had regained some of my composure. I could stand up. I told the police to make sure they took pictures of Shawn in front of the computer with that video game on it to prove that is how he died. The police went into his apartment and closed the door.

The caretaker took me to an empty apartment, so I had a private place to do what I needed to do next.

So much had happened in the last year and a half that destroyed our mother-son relationship. Shawn started having seizures again. Shawn got his own apartment. Shawn bought his own computer. Shawn stopped having contact with his family. Shawn quit taking his medications. Shawn stopped going to his doctor appointments. Unbeknownst to me, something so tragic happened in Shawn's on-line world, that he quit gaming on October 30, 2021. His real life was empty. He had left it for the game. Shawn didn't know how to come back to his real life. There was no support to help him and show him how. The withdrawal from the game became so severe, that Shawn went out and purchased a gun. Then he quit his job. All of this contributed to Shawn taking his own valuable, yet fragile life on November 20, 2021. Today I often ask myself, "How much did this Everquest game manipulate Shawn, to make those choices in the other areas of his life?" That Everquest game sucking Shawn into its fantasy world and isolating him from real life had changed my kind, funny, gentle, loving, hard-working son, into a disabled, anti-social, empty shell of a human being. I became furious! My motherly instinct immediately knew that Shawn's death had **SOMETHING** to do with that video game. Otherwise, why would he shoot himself in front of the computer, with that Everquest game on it? Shawn planned to die that way for a reason. I know Shawn was sending me a message so his death would not have to be in vain. I lost the battle to get my son, Shawn, back out of the grip of that video game.

This was Shawn's computer when I found him, with the Everquest game on it.

Right then, after the struggle that we had been through because of that video game, I also knew that the video gaming company had not heard the last from me. Little did I know then that I would be the one to continue this war.

Chapter 7: After Shawn's Death

"The darker the night - the brighter the stars, the deeper the grief – the closer to God!" Fyodor Dostoyevski

My life stopped and made a drastic detour.

The caretaker and his wife were comforting me the best they could. After I was able to recover enough from the horrifying shock of knowing that my son had killed himself my first response was to keep Shawn alive somehow. When the police came out of Shawn's apartment, after examining the scene, I asked them if we could donate Shawn's organs, so he could live on, to help someone else live better. The police said Shawn had been dead too long so the organs were not usable. The police did not know exactly when he died.

What do I do? How do I act? No one in our family had ever died by suicide before. I had never lost a child before.

I could not take any more time to be a grieving mom. I had to get myself together. Somebody had to call and inform my family and friends and tell them what happened. Someone had to make the wake and funeral arrangements. Someone had to console her grieving children. Someone had to set an example. Someone had to keep this family together the best she could. Someone had to pick up the pieces.

Time was of the essence. I had to call our priest immediately. I called Fr. Peter Szleszinski from St. Patrick's church in Hudson. I asked him to come over and pray and bless Shawn and give him the last rights, the best that he could. I desperately wanted Shawn to go to heaven and be with Jesus. Fr. Peter came and did what he could.

Then I had to figure out how to call my other children and the rest of my family. I had to tell them of this horrifying tragedy before the big dinner on Thanksgiving Day.

I already had trust issues being raised in a dysfunctional, alcoholic family. Now I felt that I couldn't even trust my own children. What if Shawn's decision to kill himself, would give one of my other children the message, that if you can't handle the pressures or stress of life, don't ask for help, just kill yourself? I was so scared. Shawn's decision to take his life has affected so many other people's lives.

The caretaker asked me who I wanted her to call for support. My daughter, Crystal who was 23 at the time, was getting ready to go to Thanksgiving dinner at my sister Maureen's. She was going to ride with Shawn and me. I needed my daughter to know that I would not be there to pick her up. I needed my daughter with me at Shawn's apartment so I asked the caretaker to call Crystal. The caretaker's daughter called and told Crystal that she needed to get to her brother's apartment as soon as possible. Crystal asked her why. She said she could not tell her and that Crystal needed to get there as quickly as possible. Crystal thought, Oh My God, something very bad has happened. Crystal got in her car and drove over to Shawn's apartment. When Crystal arrived at Shawn's apartment there were cop cars in the parking lot.

Crystal went into the building and knocked on Shawn's door. The police answered the door. She told them that this was her brother's apartment. The police sent Crystal down to the empty apartment where I was sitting.

Crystal walked into the empty apartment. I looked at her and told her Shawn was dead. We embraced and held each other for a long time.

He killed himself because of that video game.

Crystal said later, that she wasn't surprised. After she got the call from the caretaker's daughter, she knew Shawn had done something stupid. She was just glad he didn't go after me first.

Crystal cared so much about Shawn. She was sensitive to his emotional struggles because she had similar ones herself. She made time to be with him, to play with him, to let him know she loved him. This was devastating to her.

Shawn's younger brother, Tony, who was 13 at the time, was in Kentucky with his dad, Greg and Elaine. They were visiting and celebrating Thanksgiving with Elaine's family. I had to call Tony and tell him what happened. I needed him home, and he needed to be here. I called and told Greg that Shawn had killed himself. Then I asked to speak with Tony and told him what happened. Tony went numb when he heard what happened to his brother, Shawn. Tony's dad, Greg, put him on a plane the next morning, and flew him back to Minneapolis, MN. Tony was the closest to Shawn through all of this, as Tony was living with me during this whole ordeal. Tony saw how Shawn had escaped into this Everquest game rather than live his real life. Tony did not and does not to this day, play MMORPG video games because he saw how it devastated his older brother's life.

I called Shawn's older brother, Ryan, who was 25 at the time. He was in Cotton, MN with his wife and new baby, celebrating Thanksgiving dinner with Amy, a friend of his wife's. I told Ryan what had happened to Shawn. Ryan was stunned, yet not surprised. He loaded his family in the car and tried to drive home. After several miles Ryan had to turn around and go back to Amy's house because he was in shock. Eventually, several hours later, Ryan regained his composure enough to be able to make the 3-hour drive back home to Hudson, WI.

I then had to continue this most dreadful, life-changing duty of calling my sisters, my brothers and my mom, interrupting their Thanksgiving to tell them that we would not be there for Thanksgiving dinner. I had to tell them that my son, Shawn, had killed himself. We never had anyone in our family commit suicide before. This was such a shock to all of us. My brothers, sisters and my mom were all devastated. The whole family was overwhelmed with grief.

By this time the priest was done performing Shawn's last rites. The Hudson police finished their investigation. I had made all of the necessary phone calls. Crystal and I went over to my house to wait for my family to come over so we could start the grieving process together.

After hearing the news my brothers and sisters left their Thanksgiving meals and immediately came over to my house to comfort Crystal and me for the rest of the day. I was so thankful for all of my family's love, encouragement and support during this time of crisis.

I will never have a Thanksgiving meal with my "whole family" again, here on this earth.

That night I felt like I died and went to hell. I almost died in my sleep, twice. I stopped breathing. I had never done that before. I woke up gasping for air. I was so far down into the depths of despair, the depths of hell, of a mother losing her child. My spirit

92

wanted to die to be with my lost son, Shawn. I had joined the ranks of "mothers who lost a child".

I felt that I had failed as a mother knowing that my son had killed himself rather than telling me that he had bought a gun. This was the result of Shawn living only for a fantasy world. This is the epitome of where his fantasy led him. This is how disillusioned and disconnected Shawn was from the real world, from his own mother, brothers, sister and family. Part of Shawn's life is to reach out to others in his death. If you are considering hurting yourself or other people there are people willing to help you. There are people that want to help you, if you tell them what is happening in your heart and in your mind. It is my hope that my son, Shawn did not die in vain. If you need help please seek out others for support. Please do not choose a **permanent** solution, for a **temporary** problem. If Shawn were alive today, he would implore you to reach out to someone for help – a family member, a trusted one, the *National Suicide Prevention Lifeline at* 1-800-273-8255. You deserve to LIVE!

On Black Friday after Thanksgiving, November 24, it was really dark for us. We went back to Shawn's apartment. We were attempting to figure out when he died, so we could have a date of death, to give to the funeral home director. We looked on Shawn's computer. We were able to determine that he died on Tuesday, November 20. That is when the transmitting on the computer stopped. On Wednesday, November 21, I was at Shawn's apartment. He did not answer the door. He was already dead.

My children and I then went to Cullen's Funeral Home in New Richmond, WI. We needed to get our bearings as to what was going to happen next. I had never done a funeral before. Later, my mom and sister, Maureen joined us to determine when the wake and funeral would be. The funeral director thought it best that we cremate Shawn because of the amount of time that had passed since he had died. An open casket would not work. We got to see Shawn one last time, before they cremated him.

My ex-husband Bob and his wife Ellen were very kind and gracious and volunteered to help clean out Shawn's apartment and get rid of his stuff. I was in no shape to clean up and remove everything from his apartment. It was so filthy! There were empty pizza boxes stacked up in his kitchen. There were empty food containers lying all over his apartment. There was no place to sit or walk because garbage was everywhere. Bob and Ellen were at the apartment on Friday to clean up the blood, the garbage and the containers. My children and I stopped in at Shawn's apartment, after we were finished at the funeral home to see how they were doing. We gathered in a circle for a prayer. Instead, we sang "Happy Birthday" to my youngest son, Tony, as it was his birthday that day. He was 14 years old. Tony's life has forever been altered because of this tragedy.

On Saturday while I was looking on the Internet I found an article written that day about how to leave a legacy after someone dies. I loved the idea, and desperately wanted a legacy to remember my son by. I typed up forms so people could fill them out, sharing about their best memories with Shawn. At the wake and funeral, I had my children pass out the forms and ask people if they would fill them out. I then took the forms and made a book called, "A Legacy to Shawn". Later I sent a copy of his legacy to all of those who wanted one. I wished Shawn could have read it when he was alive, so he knew how much everyone liked him and cared about him. **See <u>Appendix F for Shawn's Legacy</u>**

On Saturday and Sunday my children, relatives and close friends and I spent the time going through all of Shawn's memorabilia and pictures that I had saved to make picture boards for the wake and funeral. We also picked out songs and readings for the funeral. *"Soon and Very Soon, We are Going to See the King"* by Andra'e Crouch, was my favorite song that I picked to be sung by everyone at Shawn's funeral.

Soon and Very Soon, We are Going to See the King
by Andra'e Crouch

Soon and very soon,
We are going to see the King,
Soon and very soon,
We are going to see the King.
Soon and very soon,
We are going to see the King,
Hallelujah, hallelujah,
We are going to see the King.
No more crying there,

We are going to see the King,
No more crying there,
We are going to see the King.
No more crying there,
We are going to see the King,
Hallelujah, Hallelujah,
We are going to see the King.

No more dying there,
We are going to see the King,
No more dying there,
We are going to see the King.
No more dying there,
We are going to see the King,
Hallelujah, Hallelujah;
We are going to see the King.

On Sunday evening the wake was held at the Cullen Funeral Home in New Richmond, WI. So many people came to express their condolences and offer support to my family and me. Everyone I expected was there. I know I was in my hostess mode making sure everything and everyone was all right. It kept my mind off of my own grieving, which I wasn't ready to do yet. I was very angry and hurt because my son, Shawn, was dead from choices he had made about a   video game.

The funeral was on Monday, November 26 at our church, St. Patrick's, in Hudson, WI. Father Ryan Erickson presided over the funeral. Many of Shawn's co-workers from his place of work, Papa Murphy's, attended the funeral. They shared their memories about Shawn in "Shawn's Legacy" book. I was overwhelmed with appreciation and love because they all cared so much about Shawn.

After the funeral, I still remember today, an acquaintance of the family, who had also lost a child, sharing with me, " If you think it is hard now, just wait, it is going to get a lot harder. In 3 months, 6 months, and 1 year and on, you won't have all of these people around to keep your mind off of what happened and you will never forget. The sorrow of losing a child will always be there." After all these years I have a different perspective now. It is not so much about my son, Shawn. It is about reaching out and helping others. Today when I get emails or phone calls or read an article or hear a story on the nightly news I grieve for the other mothers, the other parents, the other family members, and the other video gamers who are now going through what we went through.

I was in my "protective mother" mode for my other children. I did not want Shawn's funeral to be some dark, morbid event that would forever scar my other children's psyches. I tried to make this event somewhat light, because we know that is what Shawn would have wanted. When we were together we all just wanted to have fun. Even so, there was overwhelming grief. All of our relatives were trying to hold us together.

After the funeral, we drove to the family plot at St. Anne's cemetery in Somerset, WI. This is where Shawn's ashes were laid to rest, above his grandfather, Richard Wulf's gravesite. Note:

We did bury Shawn's ashes with one of our beloved cat's ashes, Shawn's favorite baseball cap and his rubber chicken. We tucked them all in the hole before the priest saw it because we didn't think he would approve of the chicken. (The funeral director helped with this.) We then gathered at the church for a luncheon and took time to share stories and support each other, grieving the loss of Shawn together.

After Shawn's funeral services the reality of life slapped me in the face again. I found out we had eight days to clean out his apartment, before the next month's rent was due. Again, time was of the essence. After the funeral, my children, my sister Connie and I returned to Shawn's apartment to help with the cleaning and removal of Shawn's things. I remember there were many science fiction books with demons and other dark stuff in his apartment. Ellen and I threw all of them into the dumpster. We did not want to poison anyone else's mind. I felt bad that Shawn had been living like that. That is what an addiction can do to a person's life.

Shawn's apartment was a mess. Garbage was everywhere.

There were Pizza boxes thrown all over Shawn's apartment.

Papers were all over, with notes from the video game.

I felt so betrayed and hurt by what Shawn did. I was at his apartment on Friday before Thanksgiving and he was planning to kill himself. If I only knew then, I would have tried to stop him! He did not, he would not, and he could not ask me for help. I felt that I had failed as his mother. No one else in our family had ever died by suicide. This was not in the physiological DNA of our family. We were strong, hearty survivalists. Suicide was not an acceptable choice as a conflict resolution to life for us. There was never a gun in our house and Shawn had never used a gun before. The insidious force of that Everquest video game was so powerful that it pulled him away from the DNA of our family. I am shocked and grieved that that video game warped Shawn's brain, soul and spirit so bad that this is how he ended up.

Many years later, when I think of Shawn with sadness in my heart, I am also reminded of when my beloved grandmother, Lena Cook, passed away. This had been a very sad and devastating time for our family. I was riding in the car going from her funeral to the gravesite where they would lay her in her final resting place. This song came on the radio:

Is That All There Is?

as sung by Peggy Lee

I remember when I was a very little girl, our house caught on fire
I'll never forget the look on my father's face as he gathered me up
in his arms and raced through the burning building out to the pavement
I stood there shivering in my pajamas and
watched the whole world go up in flames
And when it was all over I said to myself, is that all there is to a fire

Is that all there is, is that all there is?
If that's all there is my friends, then let's keep dancing
Let's break out the booze and have a ball
If that's all there is.

And when I was 12 years old, my father took me to circus,
the greatest show on earth
There were clowns and elephants and dancing bears
And a beautiful lady in pink tights flew high above our heads
And so I sat there watching the marvelous spectacle
I had the feeling that something was missing
I don't know what, but when it was over
I said to myself, "is that all there is to a circus?

Is that all there is, is that all there is?
If that's all there is my friends, then let's keep dancing
Let's break out the booze and have a ball
If that's all there is

Then I fell in love, head over heels in love,
with the most wonderful boy in the world
We would take long walks by the river or
just sit for hours gazing into each other's eyes
We were so very much in love

Then one day he went away and I thought I'd die, but I didn't
and when I didn't I said to myself, is that all there is to love?

Is that all there is, is that all there is?
If that's all there is my friends, then let's keep dancing

I know what you must be saying to yourselves
if that's the way she feels about it why doesn't she just end it all?
Oh, no, not me I'm in no hurry for that final disappointment
for I know just as well as I'm standing here talking to you
when that final moment comes and
I'm breathing my last breath, I'll be saying to myself

Is that all there is, is that all there is?
If that's all there is my friends, then let's keep dancing
Let's break out the booze and have a ball
If that's all there is.

Songwriters: Jerry Leiber / Mike Stoller
Is That All There Is (Remastered 2002) lyrics © Sony/ATV Music Publishing
LLC, Warner/Chappell Music, Inc.

Is that all there is to Shawn's life?

Is that all there IS?

Is THAT all there is?

How do you want your life to end up?*

The choice is yours. Please choose wisely.

*For immediate help, call the *National Suicide Prevention Lifeline
at* 1-800-273-8255

Chapter 8: From Motherhood to My Mission

"Every mom has a mission. To love, guide and protect her family. Don't mess with her while she is on it." Vicki Reece

Several weeks later there was another death in my family. My aunt unexpectedly passed away in St. Louis Park, MN on December 9, 2001 at the age of 70 years old. Aunt Theresa Wulf had been a nun in Park Rapids, MN for 15 years. This was another sad experience as I assisted in cleaning out her apartment. I was still grieving the loss of my own son, Shawn. This, however, provided some relief for me to be able to help and assist someone else in their time of need and take my mind off of my own grieving and the loss of my son.

Shawn's former boss, Bruce, from Domino's contacted his friend, Joe Winter. Joe was a newspaper reporter for the Hudson Star Observer in Hudson, WI. Bruce knew Shawn before he started playing the Everquest game and saw what happened to Shawn's life after he started playing it. Bruce suggested that Joe should write a story about what happened to Shawn to warn people that these video games are not created just for fun anymore and that they can harm people's lives.

Joe contacted me to see if I was interested in doing an interview with him to share about what happened to my son, Shawn. I agreed to do an interview with Joe, however, the timing was not right. I was not yet ready to do this. I was grieving the loss of two family members, one of which was my own son. It was the Christmas holiday season and then New Years. I was just not ready mentally and emotionally to face this type of intrusion.

This letter from Joe invited me to do the interview and the conditions/ground rules for the interview to happen.

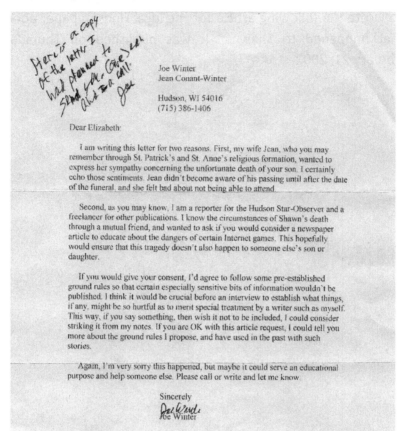

Here is a copy of the letter I had planned to send for a (one) year. Send you a call! Joe

Joe Winter
Jean Conant-Winter

Hudson, WI 54016
(715) 386-1406

Dear Elizabeth:

I am writing this letter for two reasons. First, my wife Jean, who you may remember through St. Patrick's and St. Anne's religious formation, wanted to express her sympathy concerning the unfortunate death of your son. I certainly echo those sentiments. Jean didn't become aware of his passing until after the date of the funeral, and she felt bad about not being able to attend.

Second, as you may know, I am a reporter for the Hudson Star-Observer and a freelancer for other publications. I know the circumstances of Shawn's death through a mutual friend, and wanted to ask if you would consider a newspaper article to educate about the dangers of certain Internet games. This hopefully would ensure that this tragedy doesn't also happen to someone else's son or daughter.

If you would give your consent, I'd agree to follow some pre-established ground rules so that certain especially sensitive bits of information wouldn't be published. I think it would be crucial before an interview to establish what things, if any, might be so hurtful as to merit special treatment by a writer such as myself. This way, if you say something, then wish it not to be included, I could consider striking it from my notes. If you are OK with this article request, I could tell you more about the ground rules I propose, and have used in the past with such stories.

Again, I'm very sorry this happened, but maybe it could serve an educational purpose and help someone else. Please call or write and let me know.

Sincerely
Joe Winter

After New Year's, I had several phone conversations with Joe. I was through the grieving process enough that we were finally able to meet in person at my home. In February of 2002 we met to talk about Shawn and his involvement in the Everquest game. This was my first interview about this horrible tragedy in my family's life. Joe was a very professional and kind reporter. Joe asked a lot of in-depth personal questions that made me reflect on what happened to Shawn. He helped me to begin to connect the dots. I was crying by the time the interview was over. This was just the beginning of understanding what really happened to Shawn and his video game addiction.

Joe wrote the following article for the local Hudson paper about what happened to Shawn. It was published on Thursday, February 21, 2002.

Mother seeks answers after son addicted to computer game shoots himself

Elizabeth Woolley holds a book of memories that was compiled about her son, Shawn, where dozens of contributors spoke about his sense of humor, work ethic and friendliness. "He never looked at himself that way," Woolley said. To read some of the comments, see page 5A. Photo by Joe Winter

This is the article written by Joe Winters.

A 21-year old Hudson man shot himself to death shortly after a long stint playing an Internet game to which he was addicted, and his mother is looking for answers, information and closure.

During his 12-hour stints at the computer logged on to Everquest, a role-playing game, Shawn Woolley's epilepsy was sometime triggered by the flickering screen, and the seizures on at least one occasion left his bedroom trashed.

"He preferred to have seizures and play the game because he was addicted," said Elizabeth Woolley, Shawn's mother. "He couldn't understand why I objected to him playing the game for hours on end. He couldn't understand why I was upset. Shawn had no desire to be non-addicted."

Elizabeth Woolley said the last computer screen Shawn saw still registers on his computer but to unlock that secret by entering, Woolley needs to find out his password. She currently has only his user name.

For that reason, and to investigate the possibility of a class action lawsuit against the makers of the game, Woolley has tried to telephone his Internet friends, but they are also addicted and invariably hang up on her. Woolley fears that some type of suicide pact may have been drawn up, and that there may be more victims. If there are such suicides, however, they would be scattered around the world with no logical link to connect them, so they could seem unrelated, she said.

"He didn't want to do anything, except get on the computer. Then, viola! That was his life," Woolley said, "It consumed him. Nobody could pull him back."

Many people play Everquest — some even marry their role-playing characters online — and don't get addicted. But the fact that the game can be played for hundreds of hours without any kind of resolution has brought increasing concerns about addictions such as Shawn's. Woolley said she did everything possible to get Shawn help prior to his suicide, which took place last Thanksgiving. She insisted that he have steady employment. She notes that he was well liked by his co-workers.

Woolley contacted a St. Croix County mental health care program and tried to get Shawn to reside in a group home, thinking that socialization with real people, not Everquest characters, would be beneficial. Woolley feared Shawn was becoming suicidal, but officials told Woolley that without an actual threat by Shawn, who was now an adult, they couldn't take protective action.

As part of the process, Shawn saw a psychologist. A series of medications were later prescribed for depression, seizures and being schizoid, but Shawn often wouldn't take them. When a search of Shawn's apartment was done after the suicide, not a single pill was found, she said.

Shawn lived at home for the first phase of his addiction, but he became increasingly withdrawn and wouldn't interact with family members, rather holing himself up in his bedroom. Shawn ended up getting his own apartment six months before the suicide.

"He was driving me crazy. When he was in his own place, without me to tell him to get off the computer, he was just in his perfect world, " Woolley said. "Shawn was playing constantly, and he wouldn't let me in the apartment. It looked like he hadn't cleaned it in weeks.

At one point, there were almost 300 pizza containers lying around the apartment. Rather than go shopping, which would take away from Internet play, Shawn was simply bringing home pizza from his workplace, Papa Murphy's.

Woolley last saw Shawn the Friday before the suicide, then knocked on his door the following Tuesday. Shawn wouldn't let Woolley inside and she contacted the landlord. They found a chain keeping the door shut and the landlord suggested that Woolley cut it.

"I didn't want to break in," Woolley said. "So I pounded on his windows for an hour. The next day, which was Thanksgiving and the day of the suicide, Woolley found the door with its chain had not been moved. "Then I got scared," she said. It turned out that at about 6 a.m. Shawn logged off Everquest and then shot himself.

I didn't get to say good-bye and he didn't get a chance to come to me and say he needed help." Woolley said.

Shawn bought a gun on Nov. 13. It was about that time that Shawn quit his job at Papa Murphy's. He said he had gotten another job, at Wal-Mart, which turned out not to be true.

"Shawn said that 'only my true (Everquest) friends understand me," Woolley said. When one of those friends stole some money from Shawn, he broke into tears because he felt that the person he trusted had let him down, not because of any financial loss, Woolley said.

Woolley notes that Shawn had a job he liked, family, friends and an apartment. "Shawn shunned all that for playing the game.

Shawn had stopped going to church, but toward the end some friends with whom he worked, who attend Faith Community Church, convinced him to go to church with them. Shawn had stopped believing there is a God, but

Woolley said she takes solace in knowing his new friends told Shawn there is a God who cares.

"I wasn't angry at God," Woolley said. "He's totally carrying me. There's no way I can do this without him. It's so painful."

Closure hasn't come yet for her. "It seemed to get worse. I was numb at the funeral but when that wore off it was awful." Woolley said. "I was raised to think you couldn't cry. My therapist said that crying is a gift and that you should not feel bad."

Still, Woolley said her faith continues to be strong and that she passes along faith messages to youth for whom she is a catechist at St. Patrick's Catholic Church. "I talk to them more about how important it is to have God in your life."

These are some of the memories shared about Shawn in a book compiled by his mother:

 * "Shawn was a very good and hard worker. He could bust out dishes with the best of 'em! It was nice to have him there to let me know what to do and what not to do. Shawn was a great person and he will be missed. God bless"

* "Every morning when I came to work, Shawn would always welcome me with the warmest smile and always a great joke...He will always have a special place in my heart that can never be covered or replaced."

* He was always making jokes and teasing. I worked with Shawn almost every day this summer and as I got to know him better I began to notice a politeness in him. He was becoming a friend to me and I was extremely disappointed when he stopped working at Papa Murphy's. I would love a copy of the book you make."

Right off the bat I knew that he was one of those guys who was just a nice guy who doesn't judge people before he knows them. It turned out I was right...and so much more."

For more memories from "Shawn's Legacy" go to: <u>Appendix F: Shawn's Legacy</u>

God Took Over

Things started happening in my life, that were too coincidental...I call it *God-incidental* (as quoted on July 9 of "Letting God" by A. Philip Parham). There were pieces of my life that were scattered all over. The pieces of my life were all coming together. There were 3 significant aspects of my life that are NOW totally and unequivocally connected and intertwined today. These three life experiences prepared me for the journey and battle ahead. These experiences gave me the qualifications to speak the truth about video game addiction.

First, I have experienced my own addiction. At the age of 26, I was divorced, with 3 young children. I did not want to cope in life by having another drink when things got rough, as my father had. I wanted to grow and become a better person, yet I did not know how. One day I found an "Alcoholics Anonymous (A.A.) Big Blue Book" at a garage sale and I purchased it. After reading it, I was surprised to find those people sounded a lot like me. I was relieved and excited to find there was some place I could go to learn how to live a healthy adult life. I became involved in A.A. and joined a local group. I learned so much. I learned how to apply the 12-step principles in my life in all situations. I learned how the addictive mind and personality works, thinks and manipulates others to get their drug of choice. I also went into psychotherapy for several years. Both of these things together saved my life. I never learned so much. Since then I have been on my healing/spiritual journey. I will never stop growing, because I am a life-long learner.

Second, in 1984, I decided to go back to school. I picked computer programming because my older brother, Larry, worked with computers. I thought that if Larry could do this, I could do this too. With his encouragement I took the leap of faith. I was still a single mom with 3 children, going to school full-time. I got my Associates degree in computer programming in 1986 and I started my career as a software programmer/analyst at the Hazelden Betty Ford's Drug and Alcohol Treatment Center, in Center City, MN. My latest job in computers was as a technical support representative. In my computer career of 26 years, I was trained, worked on and experienced almost every aspect of computer analysis, design, programming, implementation, upgrading and marketing on all different kinds of computer systems from main frame to Unix to DOS to MS Windows, to Apple. I know how software (including video games) is designed and created. I understand the level of detail that must be considered to create any software, what is done to enhance it, and to market it to get more customers, and keep the existing customers.

Third, I watched my son, Shawn, become addicted to the Everquest game. No other game affected him like this. I took Shawn to several professional therapists seeking help. There was none. There was no help available that I knew of! No one that I knew of had heard of video gaming addiction before this. After gaming for one and a half years, Shawn died by suicide while sitting in front of his computer, with the Everquest game on the screen. I found Shawn in his apartment on Thanksgiving morning in 2001. I experienced what video gaming addiction can do to a person's life by watching what happened to my son. Here are some working definitions of addiction:

- Between stimulus and response is our greatest power - the freedom to choose. When that freedom is gone, then it is an addiction.

- The change in a person, who becomes addicted, is based on an insight gleaned from the work of hundreds of brain researchers: **that addiction rewires the brain, dooming its owners to a downward spiral of self-defeating behavior.**

- Addiction is a behavior that is characterized by the inability to discontinue this behavior despite the negative consequences, which occur with excessive participation.

There is no difference between cocaine, heroin, alcohol, nicotine, pornography, food or video gaming addiction. All of these addictions can be a person's drug of choice. My son was living proof of that and it cost him his life.

The following article by Rachel Feltman iterates this:

The World Health Organization now recognizes video game addiction. June 18, 2018:

"Most of us understand how diseases like alcoholism and drug addiction can cause pain and suffering. Craving a cigarette or a stiff drink on occasion is one thing, but addiction forces an individual to behave in unusual—and often destructive—ways in the service of finding the next fix. But you can also become addicted to behaviors, like gambling. And medical professionals are starting to realize that in the modern age, behavioral addictions can turn seemingly harmless things—like video

games—quite dangerous.

In fact, the World Health Organization will now classify gaming disorder—an addiction to playing video games—as a real mental health condition. Reports of this change originally surfaced in December 2017, based on a beta draft released by WHO's International Classification of Diseases." Here is a link to this full article:

https://www.popsci.com/who-video-game-disorder-addiction

Here is a recent update to this groundbreaking decision:

Video game addiction is officially considered a mental disorder, WHO says

Mike Snider, USA TODAY. Published 10:12 a.m. ET May 28, 2019 | **Updated 4:40 p.m. ET May 28, 2019**

Think your kid is addicted to video games? There could be something to it.

The World Health Organization made video game addiction *an official mental health disorder. The Geneva-headquartered organization added "Gaming disorder" to the International Statistical Classification of Diseases and Related Health Problems or "ICD-11," which goes into effect in January 2022.*

The condition is included in the global medical guide within a section detailing disorders due to substance use or addictive behaviors, along with "Gambling disorder."

The ICD-11 describes "Gaming disorder" as recurrent video game playing that leads to "impaired control over gaming" and an "increasing priority given to gaming to the extent that gaming takes precedence over other life interests and daily activities," despite "the occurrence of negative consequences."....

For the full article please go to this link:

https://www.usatoday.com/story/tech/news/2019/05/28/who-officially-classifies-video-game-addiction-mental-disorder/1256352001/

I believe there is a Higher Power. I do have a spiritual life and believe that God, as I choose to call Him, had a plan for Shawn's life and for my life.

After my son died, I came to know and understand what my mission on this earth was. To offer support, encouragement and hope to those who have been affected by video gaming addiction so they do not have to go through what we went through, alone.

The following is a poem that strengthens my faith in God and reminds me that He cannot repair my broken dreams, unless I first let them go.

Let Go and Let God

As children bring their broken toys,
With tears, for us to mend,
I brought my broken dreams to God,
Because he was my friend.
But then, instead of leaving Him
In peace to work alone,
I hung around and tried to help,
With ways that were my own.
At last, I snatched them
Back and cried,
"How can you be so slow?"
"My Child," He said,
"What could I do?
You never did let go!"
- Anonymous

Now, let's put the pieces of Shawn's life together to create his legacy.

Chapter 9: Attempting To Solve The Puzzle

"Eventually all of the pieces fall into place. Until then, laugh at the confusion, live for the moment and know that everything happens for a reason." Anonymous

Do you enjoy putting jigsaw puzzles together? Have you ever sat at a table, looking at a box that had 100 pieces, 500 pieces, 1000 pieces to a puzzle? Do you find this to be fun, enjoyable or an absolute waste of time and effort? We have been on a journey to find and understand the truth of what happened in Shawn's life. It is our hope that this chapter will help us to discover the pieces and how they fit together to solve this puzzle. Here are seven major pieces of the puzzle that hopefully can help us make sense of this tragedy.

Puzzle piece # 1 – Where did the lawsuit come from?

NOTE: A special thank you needs to be expressed to Jack Thompson for his involvement in my and Shawn's life. If it weren't for him giving notoriety and credibility to my loss, it would be highly questionable if Shawn's story would have went further then our local newspaper.

Jack Thompson is a famous international lawyer from Florida who defends victims of computer games, school shootings and entertainment profanity. It just so happens that the wife of Jack Thompson is also from Hudson, WI. As a result of Joe Winter's article in the Hudson Star Observer, Jack's in-laws, who still live in Hudson, WI, read Joe's article and sent the article to their son-in-law, Jack. Jack read this article and called me to ask if I would consider filing a lawsuit against Sony Online Entertainment because of what happened to Shawn. I wanted the public to know what happened to my son and our family because of this video game. We considered filing a lawsuit to bring the public's attention to the seriousness of the addictive nature of the Everquest game. I also wanted to get access to Shawn's Everquest accounts. I needed to get a clearer picture of what was happening in Shawn's gaming life. Sony Online Entertainment would not give me the access to his account because they said there were privacy issues.

(L to R) John M. Langel Sr., Jack Thompson, Liz Woolley

After Jack Thompson agreed to become my lawyer, Stan Miller, from the Milwaukee Journal Sentinel picked up this story and did a more in-depth interview with me about what happened regarding Shawn. The article was published on March 30, 2002. Every day, I would search for Shawn's name on the internet and watch in amazement as Stan Miller's article went around the world. I did not know why so many people were interested in what happened to my son, Shawn Woolley. Stan Miller emailed me and shared that he has never had a response to anything he had written before like he received from that article.

Death of a game addict

Sucked deep into vivid fantasy cyberworld of EverQuest, ill Hudson man took own life after long hours on Web

By STANLEY A. MILLER II
of the Journal Sentinel staff

Shawn Woolley loved an online computer game so much that he played it just minutes before his suicide.

The 21-year-old Hudson man was addicted to Ever-Quest, says his mother, Elizabeth Woolley of Osceola. He sacrificed everything so he could play for hours, ignoring his family, quitting his job and losing himself in a 3-D virtual world where more than 400,000 people worldwide adventure in a never-ending fantasy.

On Thanksgiving morning last year, Shawn Woolley shot himself to death at his apartment in Hudson. His mother blames the game for her son's suicide. She is angry that Sony Online Entertainment, which owns EverQuest, won't give her the answers

"It's like any other addiction. Either you die, go insane or you quit. My son died."

Elizabeth Woolley, on her son Shawn, who played the online game EverQuest

Please see **ADDICTION, 19A**

(See **Appendix B: Complete Story about Shawn in Milwaukee Journal Sentinel**)

I started reading every response to the article that I could find and was shocked at what I read. The video gamers were pissed-off that their secret life was being exposed. The spouses, family members and loved ones were desperate for help to save their "video gamers" and their relationships.

I found out that the very thing that happened to my son Shawn was happening to thousands of other people around the world. Nobody was talking about it. It was like an underground

117

epidemic. People's lives and relationships were being ruined because of addictive video games.

Sometime later, I searched the internet to find out what others knew about video game addiction. Were there any professionals offering support for those seeking help with this addiction? I found two of them. One of them was Dr. Kimberly Young from Bradford, PA. "The pinnacle of her career was being the pioneer researcher to first identify internet addiction as a psychological condition in 1995. She was a licensed psychologist and became an internationally known expert on internet addiction. She founded the Center for Internet Addiction in 1995 and published numerous articles and books including, "Caught in the Net," the first to identify internet addiction, "Tangled in the Web," "Breaking Free of the Web," and "Internet Addiction: A Handbook and Guide for Evaluation and Treatment."

The other professional I discovered was Hilarie Cash, PhD, LMHC, CSAT. Hilarie has since founded the reSTART Life, LLC center for gaming and screen addiction in Fall City, WA. She is a great resource and tremendous encouragement in helping people and families overcome this destructive addiction.

For more support for myself, someone who had read about my story pointed me to a non-professional Yahoo Group called the Everquest Widows Group.

Dr. Laura A. Canis founded the Everquest Widows group. She was an associate professor of philosophy and department chair at Baldwin-Wallace College, Berea, Ohio. Dr. Canis had married an avid Everquest player. She said she felt like a widow. She loved her husband, Paul, dearly and did not want to split from him, so she started the Everquest Widows group, as a place to vent and know that she was not alone.

I joined the Everquest Widows Group. There was nowhere else to go for support that I knew of.

The video gaming companies are fighting this diagnosis all the way, as it might cut into their almighty profits. They are no better than drug pushers, getting their own customers addicted so they can make more money!

I posted this note in the Everquest Widows group:
https://groups.yahoo.com/neo/groups/EverQuest-Widows/conversations/topics/6885

May 17, 2002

I am looking for suggestions from everyone, as to what I can do, to help with this cause. I feel your pain, and I do not want my son to die in vain. There is help for alcoholics and other addictions. There needs to be help for this addiction.

My heart goes out to all of you, and my prayers are with you. Thank you for listening.

Sincerely, Liz

These are responses that I received from that post:

May 23, 2002 8:55 AM

Liz:
I vaguely remember reading about this tragedy months back. At least I think I did because the article mentioned your son by name. Deepest condolences on your loss. - tauceti96

May 24, 2002 4:20 AM

Dear Liz,
My deepest condolences to you.

I too am a survivor of suicide. I am a suicides daughter. Although I do not know what it's like to lose someone to the extent you have. You are in my thoughts and my Prayers. donna

---

May 24, 2002 10:57 AM

Thank you for sharing with us Liz,
My prayers go out to you and your son, peace be upon him. Your thoughts and feelings here are extremely valued. We have all had our losses, but none can compare to the tragedy you have endured. Like you, I am a programmer and I have studied EQ from the programmer aspect, wondering if it was designed in some way to create the addiction it has. Honestly, I questioned my own rationality about this, but I am relieved to see that others also question if the addiction aspects are indeed by design. I have seen the change in my wife's behavior since she first started playing EQ, and I have been at a loss to explain how the woman I so completely adored became such an irrational monster simply by playing a game.

Please Liz, stay with us here in the group and share with us your experiences, your thoughts and advice. ~Dave

---

May 29, 2002

To Liz,
My condolences on your loss dear lady....yes this is getting to be an epidemic of broken lives and relationships but as long as the money keeps pouring in Sony/Verant won't do anything about it.... Tony, Group Moderator

120

All of the posts above were of great encouragement showing love and support to me. They meant so much. My favorite response was written by Terri S., another mother of a video gamer. This is the post that inspired the title of this book:

May 23, 2002

Liz, **Your son did NOT die in vain.**

On a personal level: I am the mother of a son (21) who almost died due to health problems because of the game. I don't post often, and it's been a long time, but awhile back I posted with an update for those who knew his story. He's now in the Marines training to be an MP. He joined the USMC, before we knew about your son, out of desperation because his life was falling apart into an Everquest Black Hole.

When he came home on leave after graduating from boot camp, we discussed your tragedy. He actually cried in front of me, and then went to his room. I walked by a few minutes later and he was praying, thanking God for helping him get back to the real world, praying for his friends still addicted to Everquest, and praying for your son. He started going to church in Boot Camp, and I didn't even know!

So, now he is starting his new real-life adventure. And without a look back to the fantasy life he led, and rest assured, your son helped him to do this. My prayers are with you, and my heart-felt sympathies and appreciation. Terri

---

I have not been able to read that post without crying. I so wanted my son Shawn, to be like her son. To come out of that Everquest black hole, get back into his real life and not look back. That did not happen.

As a result of this post from Terri, I asked her to share her story of what happened to her son. Here is Terri's response:

Thursday, May 30, 2002 9:20 PM
Subject: Success Story

As per request from Liz

My son was addicted to Everquest since high school. Consequently, when he went to school he would sleep in the halls on the floor because he was up all night on EQ (Everquest) without my knowledge. Classes? Ha! Had to rest up for his next raid when he got home. He dropped out of high school. He stayed home for a year, and would get jobs, then go home sick once I went to work to play EQ. After he lost whatever job he was on currently, he would just get in his car and drive around the corner till I left.

About the time I found out how serious this was, he turned 18. I took the keyboard to work with me, and checked all activity on my computer that my limited knowledge would let me. He moved out with friends who were also EQ players. They were the only two friends he had because he would not stop playing long enough to brush his teeth, much less answer a phone call. The only friends he had left were in a place called Norrath. (Norrath is a place in Everquest.) Needless to say, he had to move back home because he didn't work while he was living in the apartment. He sold his car, his CD's, video games, almost everything he had so he could play and not go to work. That didn't last long.

When he moved back home, I said "no computer". I can go on and on how he managed to keep playing without me even knowing he had access to a computer. Picture an employee

122

shooting up three times a day at work, and no one knows how. That was my son.

The most drastic measure I took, the one that seemed to work, was to stop feeding him. He was 20 by now, and not working, so I would buy food that he didn't care much for but that would keep him alive. No snacks, no soda, no pizza, no ramen noodles (the food of choice for EQ players). I am a single mom, so I didn't have to cook big luscious meals.

He had been addicted for 3 years and his teeth were falling apart, he was skinny as a rail (before my food sabotage), he had no social life outside of EQ, no car, he was white as a ghost from lack of sun. And he stunk!

After not living in the real world for four years, and virtually no contact with anyone face to face (except me, screaming at him), he had to turn his life around. He was a high school dropout with no life other than his virtual world. And I truly believe he was dying. He joined the Marines and is at Ft. Leonard Wood right now doing his training for his Military Police MOS. He did this on his own, and I am so proud of him. I know how hard it was to walk away from his virtual life. It was all he knew. So now, when he can get to a phone, he calls me. It makes me sad that he has no other friends to call. But at least he is safe, and away from EQ. But I am happy that our relationship survived this ordeal. It almost didn't.

My one worry is that the two times he's been home on leave, he still follows the EQ message boards. He did not give up EQ willingly. I was on his back 24/7, and I used food to force him to change his life. Of course, I would have preferred him to conquer this addiction on his own. I worry daily that once he gets settled in the USMC, he will get back into the game. It seems to be very popular in the armed forces. My son is one that cannot handle the game without becoming addicted. If he gets back on the game, he may very well be discharged from the Marines.

But - finally - he is admitting he was addicted. This is a huge step. Used to be that any mention of his playing was met with anger and tantrums.

For now, I call this a success story as he is VERY happy in the USMC. He even loved Boot Camp! It was life, and he ate it up. I am crying right now with pride for him as I remember his graduation from Boot Camp. But EQ is out there, and I am worried sick that it will come back into his life again.

But, as I said, right at this time, his story is a success story.

Respectfully yours, Terri

I reflected on these responses many times. After much contemplation about this whole matter, and because of my experience with my own addiction, I understand that before any issue can be addressed, people have to start telling what is really happening. As with any addiction, if nobody knows there is a problem, nothing can be done about it. I decided to start talking and tell my story, as well as what I knew was happening to others because of addictive computer games. No one could threaten me, or make me stop telling, because I knew the truth. I had already lost my son because of his video game addiction. They couldn't take anything else that would mean so much to me anyway. So, I started doing interviews and talking with anyone who asked.

Puzzle piece # 2 – How did On-Line Gamers Anonymous® (OLGA/OLG-Anon) get started? I did not want my son to die in vain. In May of 2002, I decided to start the On-Line Gamers Anonymous® (OLGA/OLG-Anon) website www.olganon.org so others who were dealing with problems resulting from excessive video gaming, would have a place to go for support, and not be shamed. At that time there was no place I knew of to get help for video gaming addiction. Most importantly, our message boards and website would let others know that they were not alone. Hopefully we could find some tools to help each other recover from video gaming addiction. This same thing was and still is happening today, to so many others. By supporting each other we aim to help each other to get through video gaming addictions and hopefully, piece our real lives and real relationships back together.

I searched the internet to find a local web designer. I hired Angie Bendt from Wize Dezigns of Hudson, WI to help me create the website. Then I got a call from John, an ex-gamer, who wanted to volunteer to help set up the message board and make updates to the website. I accepted John's offer and he became our first webmaster.

In July of 2002, a gentlemen from the state of Florida by the name of Ron Jaffee, (Diggo McDiggity on our website) registered on our On-Line Gamers Anonymous® (OLGA/OLG-Anon) website www.olganon.org. He was the eighth person to register. Ron was a video gamer in recovery. Ron volunteered to be an administrator of our website and message boards. We gladly accepted his offer. Ron became a welcome addition to our website administration staff. He was the voice of reason and calm. He was very polite and helped make our website and organization a safe place to be. Ron helped defend me from the video gamers and defended the video gamers from me. His contribution to our organization was so great, that I believe we would not be here if it weren't for him. Ron has garnered the title of the co-founder of On-Line Gamers Anonymous® (OLGA/OLG-Anon). And so On-Line Gamers Anonymous® (OLGA/OLG-Anon) began....

Puzzle piece # 3 – Shawn and his Everquest World: As a result of the Milwaukee Journal Sentinel newspaper article, "Death of a Game Addict", word got out about what happened to my son. Some video gamers contacted me and volunteered to help me figure out what happened to Shawn in the Everquest game (I think they just wanted his "loot"). I knew nothing about Multi-Media On-line Role-Playing Games (MMORPG). I had never played one. I did not have time to play video games. The video gamers instructed me about what files to look for, and where they would be on Shawn's computer. They also shared with me that Shawn played on a Player vs. Player server called Vallon Zek. There were also Player vs. Monster servers. I learned that the Player vs. Player servers are much more violent because they are killing other players. On the Player vs. Monster servers, they are killing monsters. I was grateful for this information and was able to print all of this out to keep for evidence for a future class-action lawsuit (if necessary).

Puzzle piece # 4: What happened to the Lawsuit? On October 21, 2002, almost one year later, John Smedley, the president of Sony Online Entertainment, called me and shared with me his condolences about what happened to my son, Shawn. Even though at that time, I was in a pending lawsuit with Jack Thompson against Sony Online Entertainment I chose to speak with Mr. Smedley. I was totally innocent in this new video gaming realm. I had played games strictly for entertainment and, at that time, thought that is what video games were designed for – entertainment! I shared with Mr. Smedley about all of the responses I had read from the Milwaukee Journal Sentinel newspaper article, "Death of a Game Addict". I explained to Mr. Smedley how addicting the Everquest game was and that it was ruining people's real lives and relationships. In my ignorance, I thought I was telling Mr. Smedley something he did not know. I wanted to see what Mr. Smedley's response was to the damage that his Everquest video game was causing to real people and their families. I asked Mr. Smedley if he had a son, and he said yes. I asked Mr. Smedley how he would like it, if his son got so addicted to a game that he created, that he lost his real life and then died by suicide? Mr. Smedley responded, "he would be monitoring his son's video game playing very closely, so that would not happen."

I then asked Mr. Smedley for access to Shawn's Everquest account. Before Mr. Smedley would consider my request, Mr. Smedley asked me to get rid of my lawyer, Jack Thompson. Mr. Smedley and the executives of other video gaming companies knew of Jack Thompson and disliked him very much. The video gaming company executives were protecting their own interests because Jack Thompson was the only lawyer in the country that had the courage and conviction to stand up for morality, decency and for what is right. These executives thought of Mr. Thompson as being rude and crude. I commented to Mr. Smedley that Jack Thompson was always polite to me. I ended the conversation with Mr. Smedley and said I would get back to him about the status of my lawyer, Jack Thompson.

Jack Thompson called me and I informed him of my conversation with John Smedley, the president of Sony Online Entertainment. Mr. Thompson said that I could not talk to the enemy, and informed me that he was withdrawing from the lawsuit. I appreciate and admire Mr. Thompson and what he stands for. He is a brave man, ahead of his time, with the foresight to see the dangers of these video games to our children, families and society. It saddened me that Jack Thompson would not continue with the lawsuit.

Because of the lawsuit being withdrawn, Sony did agree to give me access to Shawn's accounts. I later found out that I was speaking to a wolf in sheep's clothing. Here are the words used by John Smedley, himself that reveals his true intentions and goals with video games. This quote is from 1999. John Smedley was acting president of Verant Interactive Inc.

> SAN DIEGO, Calif., January 26,1999 - Verant Interactive Inc. (tm), a premiere online gaming developer, announced that it has obtained the rights to Tanarus (tm), a massively multiplayer action strategy game, from 989 Studios (tm).
>
> "The acquisition of Tanarus demonstrates Verant's **commitment to the online gaming community and our intention to push Internet gaming to new heights by creating and maintaining HIGHLY ADDICTIVE, immersive and persistent gaming environments**", said John Smedley. President and CEO of Verant Interactive, Inc.

- **Read Appendix C to learn more about <u>The Birth of the Everquest Video Game</u> .**

- To learn how some video gaming companies have a "no holds barred" attitude of how to keep players on the video games read **Appendix D, Settler's Online "Monetize all weakness"**

- **Here is a current updated note about Jack Thompson:**

  In 2008, Mr. Thompson was disbarred. To learn more about Jack Thompson's fight for society, read Jack's biography, **"Out of Harm's Way"**. This book is one man's relentless crusade to topple media giants and save our children from video game madness.

  *Per Wikipedia, **John Bruce "Jack" Thompson** (born July 25, 1951) is an American activist and disbarred attorney, based in Coral Gables, Florida. Thompson is known for his role as an anti-video-game activist, particularly against violence and sex in video games.[1][2][3] During his time as an attorney, Thompson focused his legal efforts against what he perceives as obscenity in modern culture. This included rap music, broadcasts by shock jock Howard Stern, the content of computer and video games and their alleged effects on children.[4]*

  https://en.wikipedia.org/wiki/Jack_Thompson_(activist)

  Appendix E "What Happened to Jack Thompson?" contains a more in-depth article from the Game of Nerds website.

- **Here is additional information to seriously consider before bringing screens into your lives and homes.** The biggest tech figures in recent history, John Smedley, President of Sony Online Entertainment, Bill Gates, the founder of Microsoft and Steve Jobs, the founder of Apple raised their children technology free or tech-limited. These technology experts send their children to schools with zero technology. Bill and Melinda Gates did not give their children cell phones until they were 14 years old and wish they had waited longer. Tech-savvy Mark Cuban, a judge on Shark Tank, has a router so he can see what his children are doing on-line. He can also shut them down, if need be. This ought to be a huge red flag about the dangers of the abuses of video gaming and technology to the rest of us parents and society, who are raising children around the world. These most important men who work(ed) in technology and with video gaming systems do not allow or limit their own children's playing of video games. If these worldwide computer gurus know the dangers, why don't they warn the rest of us about the addictive power of digital technology?

This is a summary of an article written for Business Insider by Chris Weller on January 10, 2018.

"Bill Gates and Steve Jobs raised their kids tech-free — and it should've been a red flag". *Psychologists are quickly learning how dangerous smartphones can be for teenage brains.*

Research has found that an eighth-grader's risk for depression jumps 27% when he or she frequently uses social media. Kids who use their phones for at least three hours a day are much more likely to be suicidal. And recent research has found the teen suicide rate in the US now eclipses the homicide rate, with smartphones as the driving force.

But the writing about smartphone risk may have been on the wall for roughly a decade, according to educators Joe Clement and Matt Miles, coauthors of the recent book "Screen

Schooled: Two Veteran Teachers Expose How Technology Overuse is Making Our Kids Dumber."

It should be telling, Clement and Miles argue, that the two biggest tech figures in recent history — Bill Gates and Steve Jobs — seldom let their kids play with the very products they helped create.

"What is it these wealthy tech executives know about their own products that their consumers don't?" the authors wrote. The answer, according to a growing body of evidence, is the addictive power of digital technology...."

Here is the link to the full article:

http://www.businessinsider.com/screen-time-limits-bill-gates-steve-jobs-red-flag-2017-10

Puzzle piece # 5: What happened to Shawn in the game? After gathering all of the evidence, this is my hypothesis of what I believe happened to Shawn.

In the beginning, I thought maybe Shawn and some other gamers had made a suicide pact, and all killed themselves on the same day or something crazy like that (i.e. Jimmy Jones People's Temple mass suicide of November, 1978 in Guyana or Heaven's Gate religious group in March, 1997 in San Diego, CA). Or possibly something happened the day that he died, in the game, and he reacted to it, by killing himself.

Another piece of information that Shawn's sister, Crystal, shared shortly after he died: **"Recently, I was driving him home and we were talking about how he was doing. He revealed that there was someone that he loved and that touched me. He never**

talked about that much and I was happy to know that he was
capable of feeling love."

As you will soon see, this comment validated what we were
soon to find out.

Liz, getting in Shawn's Everquest accounts,
with Ron's help. 2002.

Almost one year later, in October 2002, after receiving access to
Shawn's accounts from John Smedley of Sony Online
Entertainment, our co-founder and administrator, Ron J. (Diggo
McDiggity on our website www.olganon.org) volunteered to fly
up from Florida to Wisconsin. Ron spent the week helping me
solve the dark mystery of what happened to Shawn in the
Everquest game.

Ron and I set up Shawn's computer in my living room to start
our investigation. Once Ron and I logged into Shawn's Everquest
account, I saw this character called ILUVEYOU, created in
Shawn's own image. I burst into tears. I was not expecting to
find out that "love" was a factor behind his death.

Shawn's "iluveyou" character in the game.

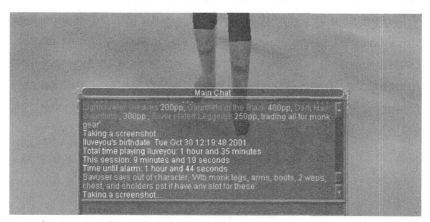

Main Chat

Lightbracer Greaves 200pp, Gauntlets of the Black 400pp, Dark Mail
Gauntlets, 300pp , Silver plated Leggings 250pp, trading all for monk
gear
Taking a screenshot...
Iluveyou's birthdate: Tue Oct 30 12:19:48 2001.
Total time playing Iluveyou: 1 hour and 35 minutes
This session: 9 minutes and 19 seconds
Time until alarm: 1 hour and 44 seconds
Savuser says out of character, Wtb monk legs, arms, boots, 2 weps,
chest, and sholders pst if have any slot for these'
Taking a screenshot...

In the screenshot above, you can see the stats from Shawn's Iluveyou character.

Shawn had played on Vallon Zek server since he started playing the Everquest game in February of 2000 . Ron and I found that on October 30, 2001, Shawn created the character called ILUVEYOU, in his own image on the Vallon Zek server. Shawn used that ILUVEYOU character for one hour and 35 minutes on

October 30, 2001. I am guessing that Shawn shared his romantic feelings with someone in the game, and the response was so horrifying, that my son quit playing the Everquest game that day. I was not aware that Shawn had quit playing that video game that day. He left the Vallon Zek server that day, (the server he had been on since he started playing that video game in February 2000). He never went back on that server again and never used the ILUVEYOU character again.

Shawn was at a point in his life, where he was having difficulties with real-life relationships. He blended his real life in Hudson, WI and his fantasy life on the Everquest game so much that he could not distinguish between the two. Shawn was so invested in his digital relationship that he became very vulnerable. Apparently his love life in the game was not a fantasy to him. Whatever happened in that encounter with that other person in the Everquest game on October 30, 2001 so deeply hurt Shawn, that it became the final betrayal for Shawn in his real and fantasy life. The withdrawal from the game and the fantasy relationship became so severe for Shawn that on November 13, 2001, he went out and purchased a 22 rifle from Wal-Mart.

We found the receipt for the purchase of the 22-rifle when we cleaned out Shawn's apartment.

After Ron and my investigation into Shawn's accounts, this is a partial response that Ron wrote to John Smedley:

"I just wanted to take a minute to thank you for the help you've given Liz so far.

I just flew back home to Orlando this evening after spending countless hours over the past few days going through Shawn's PCs, personal notes, and pages of hastily scribbled Locs, trade skill recipes and other EQ-related papers, looking

for answers. While I don't believe we found any
specific information that we didn't know before, we were able
to answer some questions and start filling in the time-line
between his first install of EQ in February of 2000 and his last
day in November of 2001.

The character restores were helpful in this regard and I think
Liz's seeing her son's characters gave her a better idea of how
Shawn spent his final months, as I explained a bit about his
character's classes and abilities, and how that type of
character functions in Norrath."

I am so thankful to Ron for making the sacrifice of his finances and time to come up from Florida to go through all of Shawn's papers and notes to help piece this puzzle together.

I never did meet any of Shawn's friends in the Everquest game. Maybe you could help me. Shawn played on the Vallon Zek server in Everquest, from February 2000 to the end of October 2001. His character names were: blofeld, soandso, xebanis, aquatik, geriatrik, krabastik, xsattilya,   wiggum_r, bobastik, chabasis, chocco, geriatrik, Iluveyou, niktikie, nismaten, putang, puttnam, quillik, saal, salaldil, woolley.

Here is a list of Shawn's friends for his character **chabassis:** refatin, chaot, dmex, sasisu, nbkan. Here is a list of his friends for his character **chocco:** biaxil, urthern, occuler, aabrum, furburll, animed, strydaar, latalon, ellrathan, talonsaldar, atarax, heeduhh, puinsai, bublezx, qooli, zozi. Here is a list of his friends for his character **putang:** nuddas, escade, pumo, aabrum, occuler, urthern, biaxil, animed, latalon, talonsaldar, atarax, heeduhh, puinsai, phargan, azae, zozi, qooli, tupadre, bublez. Here is his friends for his character **quillik:** talonsaldar, latalon, qooli, puinsai, phargan, zozi, heeduhh. Here is his list of friends for his character **woolley:** talonsaldar, latalon, qooli, puinsai, phargan, zozi, heeduhh, animed, occuler, cybernine.

If you were a player in the Everquest game, do you know of any of the above listed "characters"? If you knew Shawn in the Everquest game, or any of these characters, please feel free to contact me.

Puzzle piece # 6: What was the significance of Shawn's apartment number being 104? In 2013, while doing an

interview about Shawn, I had to look up some papers about him. While doing that, I saw the number 104 written on his address. My first thought was, why is that number there? By then, I had completely forgotten what his address was. I shuffled through more of his papers to verify that yes, his apartment in Hudson was number 104. In 2009, the World Headquarters of On-Line Gamers Anonymous® was established in Pennsylvania. The address of the headquarters is 104 Street Name. When I connected these two dots, I was like, oh my God! Shawn is still with us! What another God-incident! **See <u>Appendix G: Events of Shawn's Life, in Chronological Order</u>**

Shawn's apartment door (2001).   **On-Line Gamers Anonymous® HQ.**

The final puzzle piece # 7: Can I forgive? As I was writing this book with the help and encouragement from my friend John, he asked me if I had met any of these gamer friends of Shawn's in real life. I replied "No, but I would love to." John asked if I had a picture of the female friend, who Shawn had professed his love to with his "Iluveyou" character. I said "No, I did not know who she was". I then said "that is one gamer friend of Shawn's who I would never want to meet." John asked, "Liz, if you met this gamer friend, what would you do?" I replied, "I would want to know what she said to my son that was so repulsive that my son would leave his gaming life and never go on that server again." (I believe it was a man behind a woman character because at that time in the Everquest game, there weren't many women actually playing that game. Most of the women characters were really men because you could be anyone you wanted to be in the games. You could also do and say anything to anyone that you wanted because you were anonymous and no one would ever know who you really were). John suggested that I forgive this person. For the first time since my son died this was presented to me. Can I forgive this person who hurt and betrayed Shawn so badly that he ended up taking his own life? "How I forgive others, is how God will forgive me." "Forgive and I shall be forgiven." It is not easy to forgive someone who has caused so much pain, hurt and anguish in my life. Can I do that? Forgiving someone is such a powerful experience. Show me God, how to forgive this person, the way you forgive me. Forgiveness is a miracle. Both to accept forgiveness and to give forgiveness. Is there somebody in your life that you need to forgive? Is there someone that you need to ask for forgiveness from?

We believe that if you take the time and effort to put this puzzle together, you will understand better the challenges some people who are affected by video game or tech addiction (be it the addict or his/her family members) go through trying to experience a productive, fulfilling quality of life.

Chapter 10: Closing Thoughts

"God, give me grace to accept with serenity the things that cannot be changed, courage to change the things that ought to be changed and the wisdom to distinguish the one from the other." Reinhold Niebuhr

Let us take time to reflect on this journey that we have been on together, so far. We started out with an examination of Shawn's life and "Let the Games Begin". We have shared some incredible experiences of life and a moment of death.

I hope this time invested together has been both an encouragement and a challenge to you. Now we are at a pivotal junction. We are ratcheting up this conversation to seriously examine where we are going and why. We are determining what the future for each reader - each family - each community holds and how we choose to live. I hope you are ready because the game of life just got real intense!

Have you ever felt your life ugly, worthless or crude? No value left, all desire gone? Where do you see your life headed? Has everybody given up on you? We haven't, and neither has God. It is our hope and prayer that these words, stories and information have been both encouraging and challenging to you. The fight is never over until you say so. It's our desire that Shawn's death was not in vain. You are part of that equation now. This book is about you and the choices that you will make going forward. Whether you are a video gamer, a loved one of a video gamer or a "concerned citizen", we hope you will go to our website (www.olganon.org), register and join us in this movement.

The following poem demonstrates how our life can change when we are in the hands of our Creator. How one touch from Him can make all the difference in our lives. Never give up and keep on being.

The Touch of the Masters Hand

Myra 'Brooks' Welch

T'was battered and scarred, and the auctioneer thought it scarcely worth his while to waste much time on the old violin, but held it up with a smile; "What am I bidden, good folks," he cried, "Who'll start the bidding for me?" "A dollar, a dollar"; then two! "Only two? Two dollars, and who'll make it three? Three dollars, once; three dollars twice; going for three.."

But no, from the room, far back, a gray-haired man came forward and picked up the bow; Then, wiping the dust from the old violin, and tightening the loose strings, he played a melody pure and sweet as caroling angel sings.

The music ceased, and the auctioneer, with a voice that was quiet and low, said; "What am I bid for the old violin?" And he held it up with the bow. A thousand dollars, and who'll make it two? Two thousand! And who'll make it three? Three thousand, once, three thousand, twice, and going and gone," said he. The people cheered, but some of them cried, "We do not quite understand what changed its worth." Swift came the reply: "The touch of a master's hand."

And many a man with life out of tune, and battered and scarred with sin, Is auctioned cheap to the thoughtless crowd, much like the old violin, A "mess of pottage," a glass of wine; a game - and he travels on. "He is going" once, and "going twice, He's going and almost gone." But the Master comes, and the foolish crowd never can quite understand the worth of a soul and the change that's wrought by the touch of the Master's hand.

YouTube video of this song/poem
https://www.youtube.com/watch?v=mTsjZ_DKtp8

In examining and evaluating the value of your life, take a moment and look at yourself and what you have become. Are you connected with your own life? Your spouse? Your children? Your family? Your friends? Your community? Your place of worship? Are you physically healthy? What about your finances? Where do you want to be in a year? 5 years? 10 years? A husband shared this on the olganon.org website: *"If you are in a relationship, and you have a choice between playing video games or being with people, choose being with people. You can't replace people once you have alienated them from your life and they are gone. It's not worth it."* The only hope we have is to believe in God. Only God can change a heart. Choose wisely.

Below is another story about the true meaning of life. There is more to the world then what you physically see with your eyes. We have so much to be thankful for.

A final note about the Seven Wonders of this World....

*A group of students in a high school were asked to list what they thought were the present **"Seven Wonders of the World,"***

Though there were some disagreements in the papers, the following received the most votes:

1. Egypt's Pyramids	*5. Empire State Building*
2. Taj Mahal	*6. St. Peter's Basilica*
3. Grand Canyon	*7. China's Great Wall*
4. Panama Canal	

While gathering the votes, the teacher noted that one quiet student hadn't turned in her paper yet. So she asked the girl if she was having trouble with her list.

The girl replied, "Yes, a little. I couldn't quite make up my mind because there were so many."

The teacher said, "Well, tell us what you have, and maybe we can help."

The girl hesitated, then read, "I think the 'Seven Wonders of the World' are:

1. To see	*5. To feel*
2. To hear	*6. To laugh*
3. To touch	*7. And to love.*
4. To taste	

The room was so quiet you could have heard a pin drop. Many of the things we overlook as being simple and ordinary and take for granted, are truly wondrous!

A gentle reminder to all of us - the most precious things in life cannot be built by hand or bought by man or found in video games.

This story was originally told by Joy Garrison Wasson, an English teacher in Muncie, Indiana for over 30 years.

Use this link to see this on video.
https://www.youtube.com/watch?v=IFpBehVB1Zc

Another favorite quote of ours is *"Our life is God's gift to us, What we do with our life is our gift to God"* by Leo Buscaglia. If you are reading this book right now, you have been given this incredible gift called life! We all look at the past and see screw-ups, poor choices, missed opportunities, bad investments. Some of us also have wonderful, caring, loving relationships. Some of us did our best in school. Some of us have great careers and tremendous families. Right now at this very moment, you can make a choice to share with someone that you love them. You can make the choice to forgive someone, to set yourself free. You can choose to get help for an addiction that you have or encourage someone who needs help.

For each reader, here is something to consider/ponder about the theme of this book, "**YOUR SON DID NOT DIE IN VAIN!**". One of my all-time favorite books to read is titled "In His Steps" by Charles Sheldon. This book is a Christian classic published in 1896 that has sold over 30 million copies. It was this book that was the catalyst for the popular accessory bracelet and movement in the 1990's – WWJD – What Would Jesus Do? I would like for you to think about the following application for the title of this book. When you are facing a choice in your life, whether big or small, between good and bad, right or wrong; ask yourself this, "Do I want to do this for my own selfish gain and pleasure or do I need to do this because I love God?" If you chose for your own selfish gain and pleasure, then ask yourself if you can look heavenward and say to "Our Heavenly Father"...**Your Son did NOT die in vain**. Hopefully by making this statement, it will change your perspective of what to do. I believe if you are looking for courage and need some extra strength, make this statement to "Our Heavenly Father", **Your Son did NOT die in vain** and see what happens. Listen and wait for the Holy Spirit as He guides and directs you in the choices you will make. I believe making this statement, **Your Son did NOT die in vain**, for people who are Christian has incredible potential to deepen your love and obedience to "Our Heavenly

Father". May you take the challenge to use this tool to change your life.

In conclusion, the motto of Outreach for the On-Line Gamers Anonymous® organization is:

Gaming is your business... Quitting is ours!

This book is part of a series produced by OLGA/OLG-Anon/Outreach Online Gamers Anonymous® World Services for the benefit of the addicted video gamer, family members, loved one, friend, concerned others and those who inform and reach out to others. The next book will further address why video games are no longer created just for fun. Video games can be toxic and addictive to a person's real life and relationships. There is also an in-depth chapter of suggestions of "What Can Be Done".

We would love to hear your comments, insights, questions, and recommendations about this book and/or anything else about video game or technology addiction. Please contact us at:
On-Line Gamers Anonymous®
Email: olga@olganon.org
Web Site: www.olganon.org
Hot-Line: 612-245-1115
OLGA® for recovering video gamers
OLG-Anon for family members, friends, loved ones, concerned others
Outreach for those who inform and reach out to others

For booking and speaking engagements, please contact:
John M. Langel Sr.
Executive Director of Outreach for On-Line Gamers Anonymous®
Outreach for those who inform and reach out to others
Phone: 717-329-5494
Email: john@olganon.org
Web Site: www.olganon.org

Appendices

Appendix A: Sample of Shawn's work

This is a paper Shawn wrote in 1997 for his Junior year writing class at Osceola High School about gambling (somewhat prophetic I thought, as it is very close to video gaming….). This piece also illustrates Shawn's natural wit, which he transfers into his writing:

Gambling Fever

It's Little Miss Prissy and Mr. Ed coming around the bend, neck and neck, all of a sudden, from out of nowhere, comes Silver Lightning from behind and cuts to the inside to defeat them. Oh my God folks, what an exciting race. Silver Lightning is the winner, with Mr. Ed placing in at 2nd, and Little Miss Prissy coming in at third. I don't know about you people, but I was on the edge of my seat there.

This is very typical reaction at a horse race. Horseracing is a very popular type of gambling. Gambling has been and probably will always be an American tradition. When did gambling become popular in North America? What are the five types of gambling, and what is compulsive gambling?

The history of gambling goes back to the time of Colonial America. The most common form back then was lotteries. They held lotteries mainly to help pay for things like reconstruction after a war and building new towns. When England made the Stamp Act, which helped cause the American Revolution, it put a one-shilling tax on playing cards. This angered the colonists as much as the tax on tea.

During the 1840's, a reforming spirit swept across the Unites States. Many societies formed to protest the use of swearing, and even the moving of mail on Sunday. Many people attacked gambling because so many lotteries were run by people who stole the money and left town. Reformers also felt that many people who bought tickets could not afford them and bought them instead of taking care of their families. As a result of these reform efforts, most states began to outlaw lotteries. By 1860, every state in the nation except Delaware, Kentucky, and Missouri had passed laws making lotteries and many other forms of gambling, illegal.

That did not mean that gambling disappeared. Gambling took place openly in such cities as New York, Chicago, and New Orleans. The police were often paid to look the other way while illegal gambling continued. For some people, the fact that gambling was illegal made it more exciting.

Between 1900 and 1917, a reform-minded group called the "Progressives" worked very hard to stop corruption and dishonest behavior in business and government. They attacked things they considered morally wrong, such as drinking and gambling. As a result, most states outlawed gambling.

Of all the types of gambling, bingo, by far, is the most common form of legal gambling. The most favorite, though, would have to be lotteries and casinos.

When most people think of casinos, they imagine the casinos of Las Vegas or Atlantic City. In 1993, Americans spent about $297.3 billion in casino games and slot machines, which is the most money ever spent on one type of gambling. Then there is the lottery, which is a game in which the players buy a numbered ticket and hope to win a prize if their number is the one drawn from among all of those who have bought tickets for the lottery. The lotteries you all are most familiar with are

Powerball, Gopher 5, Megabucks, Daily Millions and the Daily 3. These are all run by the state, which you know take a good little chunk out.

Pari-mutuel and off-track betting are almost the same thing. Pari-mutuel betting is when you choose which horse or dog is going to win at the race. Off-track betting is when you go to some place other than the track and place your bet.

For most people who bet, gambling is a form of recreation and fun. An evening playing poker or bingo is merely entertainment. For some people, however, gambling is a compulsion, a disease they cannot control. One evening at the racetrack is not enough. They gamble and keep on gambling until they have nothing left and even then they try to get money just so they can gamble it away. These people may become addicted to gambling and it may take control of their behavior. These people have a disorder known as compulsive gambling. They have groups to help these people sort of like Alcoholics Anonymous or AA. Like AA the Gamblers Anonymous group have a 12-step program to help them through. Like alcoholism, the addiction may destroy their lives. Are you a compulsive gambler? Ask yourself these questions. If you answer yes to at least 5 of these questions you may be a compulsive gambler. Now, I know you all are too young to gamble a lot, but if you think a friend or relative may be a compulsive gambler, here are some signs to look for.

Now that I've told you the different types of gambling, it's history, and what it can do to you if you're not careful. I hope you have a better understanding of it, I know that I'm not old enough to legally gamble, but when I am, I am going to go to a casino. And the first place I'm heading for is the buffet line.

Appendix B: Story about Shawn in Milwaukee Journal Sentinel

By Stanley A. Miller II

Published on March 30, 2002

Death of a game addict

Sucked deep into vivid fantasy cyberworld of EverQuest, ill Hudson man took own life after long hours on Web

By STANLEY A. MILLER II
of the Journal Sentinel staff

Shawn Woolley loved an online computer game so much that he played it just minutes before his suicide.

The 21-year-old Hudson man was addicted to EverQuest, says his mother, Elizabeth Woolley of Osceola. He sacrificed everything so he could play for hours, ignoring his family, quitting his job and losing himself in a 3-D virtual world where more than 400,000 people worldwide adventure in a never-ending fantasy.

On Thanksgiving morning last year, Shawn Woolley shot himself to death at his apartment in Hudson. His mother blames the game for her son's suicide. She is angry that Sony Online Entertainment, which owns EverQuest, won't give her the answers

> "It's like any other addiction. Either you die, go insane or you quit. My son died."
>
> **Elizabeth Woolley**, on her son Shawn, who played the online game EverQuest

Please see **ADDICTION, 19A**

Sucked into vivid fantasy cyberworld of Everquest, ill Hudson man took own life after long hours on Web

Shawn Woolley loved an online computer game so much that he played it just minutes before his suicide.

The 21-year-old Hudson man was addicted to Everquest, says his mother, Elizabeth Woolley of Osceola. He sacrificed everything, so he could play for hours, ignoring his family, quitting his job and losing himself in a 3-D virtual world where more than 400,000 people worldwide adventure in a never-ending fantasy.

On Thanksgiving morning last year, Shawn Woolley shot himself to death at his apartment in Hudson. His mother blames the game for her son's suicide. She is angry that Sony Online Entertainment, which owns Everquest, won't give her the answers she desires.

She has hired an attorney who plans to sue the company in an effort to get warning labels put on the games.

"It is like any other addiction," Elizabeth Woolley said last week. "Either you die, go insane or you quit. My son died."

In the virtual world of Everquest, players control their characters though treasure-gathering, monster-slaying missions call quests. Success makes the characters stronger as they interact with other players from all over the real world.

Woolley has tried tracing her son's Everquest identity to discover what might have pushed him over the edge. Sony Online cites its privacy policy in refusing to unlock the secrets held in her son's account.

She has a list of names her son scrawled while playing the game: "Phargun." "Occulaer." "Cybernine." But Woolley is not sure if they are names of online friends, places he explored in the game or treasures his character may have captured in quests.

"Shawn was playing 12 hours a day, and he wasn't supposed to because he was epileptic, and the game would cause seizures," she said. "Probably the last eight times he had seizures were because of stints on the computer.

Woolley knows her son had problems beyond Everquest, and she tried to get him help by contacting a mental health program and trying to get him to live in a group home. A psychologist diagnosed him with depression and schizoid personality disorder, symptoms of which include a lack of desire for social relationships, little or no sex drive and a limited range of emotions in social settings.

"This fed right into the Everquest playing," Woolley said. "It was the perfect escape."

Vulnerable to addiction

Jay Parker a chemical dependency counselor and co-founder of Internet/Computer Addiction Services in Redmond, WA. *said Woolley's mental health problems put him in a category of people more likely to be at risk of getting addicted to online games.*

Parker said people who are isolated, prone to boredom, lonely or sexually anorexic are much more susceptible to becoming addicted to online games. Having low self-esteem or poor body image are also important factors, he said.

"The manufacturer of Everquest purposely made it in such a way that it is more intriguing to the addict," Parker said. "It could be created in a less addictive way, but (that) would be the difference between powdered cocaine and crack cocaine."

Parker doesn't make the narcotics analogy lightly. One client - a 21-year-old college student – stopped going to class within eight weeks after he started playing Everquest his senior year.

After playing the game for 36 hours straight, he had a psychotic break because of sleep deprivation, Parker said.

"He thought the characters had come out of the game and were chasing him," Parker said. "He was running through his neighborhood having hallucinations. I can't think of a drug he could have taken where he would have disintegrated in 15 weeks.

Common warning signs

There are several questions people who think they are addicted to computers and the Internet can ask themselves to see whether they might have a problem, Parker said, including whether they can predict the amount of time they spend on the computer or have failed trying to control their computer use for an extended period of time.

Parker said that any traumatic setback to Shawn Woolley's character in Everquest could have traumatized an already vulnerable young man.

It may be that the character was slain in combat and Woolley had trouble recovering him. Or, he could have lost a treasured artifact or massive wealth, or been cast out of one of the game's social clubs, called guilds.

"The social component is big because it gives players a false sense of relationships and identity," Parker said. "They say they have friends, but they don't know their names."

Elizabeth Woolley remembers when her son was betrayed by an Everquest associate he had been adventuring with for six months.

Shawn's online brother-in-arms stole all the money from his character and refused to give it back.

"He was so upset, he was in tears," she said. "he was so depressed, and I was trying to say, "Shawn, it's only a game." I said he couldn't trust those people.

Sony Online Entertainment declined to comment for this story, but Everquest fans say the game is a fun diversion that is much better than watching television.

Donna Cox of Schaumburg, Ill., has played for about two years and enjoys the adventuring and socializing. Cox and her husband, Bob, play together and team up against the game's challenges.

It's like an adult playground," said Donna Cox, a professional who manages a team of computer programmers. "You can become anything you want. People only see the side of you that you want them to see."

Cox played about 40 hours a week at the height of her gaming but now plays only a couple of times a week. "Once you get into the high-end game, it takes a lot of time," she said.

Dody Gonzales of Milwaukee has played the game for about three years and has more than a dozen characters spread across the Everquest realm. Gonzales, who plays about four hours a night, knows Everquest has been blamed for people's problems because it's a topic discussed in the online community.

Said player Vincent Frederico of Rochester, N.Y.: "It's almost like a drug. If you are not happy with your real life, you can always go in...Someone who lacks social skills, they could find it much easier just to play the game instead of going out to a bar."

A game without an end: Everquest
How does it pull people in?

One key component is that the game can be played indefinitely, and there are always people populating the online world. Everquest and other online games also have a social structure.

"The graphics are absolutely thrilling. They just haul you in," said Parker, who has treated several people for Everquest addiction. "The other piece is that it takes time to leave the game. You have to find a place to hide to get out, and that makes people want to play   longer."

For people who are unhappy, socially awkward or feel unattractive, online games provide a way to reinvent themselves.

Shawn Woolley – who was overweight, worked in a pizza restaurant and lived alone in an apartment the last months of his life – may have depended on Everquest to provide the life he really wanted to live.

"People like to create new personas," Parker said. "You see a lot of gender-bending."

Hooked on 'EverCrack'

Interest in online games grew in 1997 with Origin Systems' Ultima Online, now with about 225,000 players. Microsoft's Asheron's Call, with around 100,000 subscribers, provides a virtual world similar to Everquests. Most online games require an initial software purchase pus monthly fee of about $10.

The games have roots in Dungeons & Dragons, the role-playing game created in 1974 by TSR Games in Lake Geneva. But D&D requires human contact to play; its digital counterparts do not.

David Walsh, president of the National Institute on Media and the Family in Minneapolis, said many Everquest players refer to it as "Evercrack".

Walsh who didn't know the details of Woolley's suicide, thinks mental health problems linked to playing online games, especially Everquest, are growing.

"Could a person get so engrossed that they become so distressed and distraught that it could put them over the edge?" Walsh said, "It probably has something to do with the game. But you average person or average gamer won't do this. It's a coming together of a number of circumstances.

Walsh and Parker both said online games as a whole are not inherently bad, and Walsh compared playing online games to drinking alcohol. Both can be harmful if abused.

"I've seen a lot of wreckage because of Everquest," Parker said. "But they are all the same. It's like cigarettes. They need to come with a warning label. 'Warning, extensive playing could be hazardous to your health."

Warning labels are exactly what Jack Thompson, a Miami attorney and vocal critic of the entertainment industry, wants to result from a lawsuit he plans to file against Sony Online Entertainment for Elizabeth Woolley.

"We're trying to whack them with a verdict significantly large so they, out of fiscal self-interest, will put warning labels on," he said. "We're trying to get them to act responsibly. They know this is an addictive game."

"I am sure we are going to find things akin to the tobacco industry memos where they said nicotine is addictive," he said. "There is a possibility of a class action lawsuit."

John Kircher, a professor at Marquette University Law School, and expert in personal injury law, said a negligence action might be won if plaintiffs could successfully argue Everquests publishers "should have foreseen an unreasonable risk of harm, that people could potentially hurt themselves.

"Then there is the issue of First Amendment rights," Kircher said. "Does the First Amendment right trump the rights of the plaintiff? If the Internet is a form of publication . . . there is a balance the courts try to strike, and it's not an easy question."

Journal Sentinel correspondent Joe Winter contributed to this story.

Appendix C: The Birth of the Everquest Video Game

Are video games addictive? Can they become a drug of choice for some? Here is an article, written in 1999 about the intentional addictive design of Tanarus, the forerunner to Everquest. At the time this article was written, John Smedley was the acting president of Verant Interactive. John Smedley is now the president of Sony Online Entertainment the creators of Everquest.

By Kathryn Balint, Copley News Service

SAN DIEGO, Calif., January 26, 1999 - Verant Interactive Inc. (tm), a premiere online gaming developer, announced that it has   obtained   the rights to Tanarus (tm), a massively multiplayer action strategy game, from 989 Studios (tm).

*"The acquisition of Tanarus demonstrates Verant's commitment to the online gaming community and our intention to push Internet gaming to new heights by creating and maintaining highly addictive, immersive and persistent gaming environments", said **John Smedley. President and CEO of Verant Interactive, Inc.***

Members of Verant Interactive staff were on the original development team for Tanarus at 989 Studios and have maintained the product since its launch.

"We are extremely pleased with the acquisition of Tanarus and are planning a series of new promotions and enhancements to insure it remains one of the best online games on the Net", said Russell Shanks, Verant's Chief Technology Officer and Producer of Tanarus.

Tanarus has been heralded by reviewers as "HIGHLY ADDICTIVE" and "an example of what Internet gaming should be about". Featuring multiple cities, a variety of completely customizable lethal tanks and unmatched team play, Tanarus pits players spanning the globe against each other in a real time battle to control cities through teamwork and heavy firepower. Fighting in ever-changing, dynamic battlefields that range from post-apocalyptic cities to industrial wastelands, players have more than 30 different weapons and modules at their disposal.

Tanarus supports Microsoft's Direct3D API, supported by a number of 3D chipsets, including Voodoo Graphics by 3Dfx Interactive.

Verant Interactive is an independent development studio that develops cutting-edge online games. Based in San Diego, California, Verant Interactive has a staff of 70 employees who consist of the development teams responsible for the online games Tanarus and EverQuest.

In 2000, Sony Online Entertainment purchased Verant. Here is an article written about that purchase:

Sony Acquires On-line Video Gaming Company Verant Interactive

By **Rick DeMott** |

Friday, June 16, 2000 at 12:00am

Sony Pictures Entertainment (SPE) announced it has acquired the on-line game company Verant Interactive, Inc. and named digital gaming executive Kelly Flock as president and CEO of Sony Online Entertainment. *Verant will be blended into* Sony Online Entertainment, *which will base its operations in San Diego, California. The new arm of Sony has been responsible*

158

for operating the popular on-line games EVERQUEST, TANARUS and SOVEREIGN. **Verant President John Smedley will become Sony Online Entertainment's executive vice president and chief operating officer.**

Here is the link for the full article:
https://www.awn.com/news/sony-acquires-line-gaming-company-verant-interactive

"That emotional involvement keeps pulling people back, which was the result that the EverQuest team had intended. One of the video game's developers, Geoffery Zatkin, was hired because he has a degree in psychology and was experienced with online communities."

Jay Parker a chemical dependency counselor and co-founder of Internet/Computer Addiction Services in Redmond, WA. said *"The manufacturer of Everquest purposely made it in such a way that it is more intriguing to the addict. It could be created in a less addictive way, but (that) would be the difference between powdered cocaine and crack cocaine."*

Appendix D: Settlers Online Dev: "Monetize all weakness"

The following is a portion of an article from the internet about psychological hooks purposely put in the video games. **A recent phenomenon in the Fortnite video game, debuted in 2017 uses several of the principles described below to exploit the customers in their video game. Fortnite is a free video game to get you started, and once hooked, you cannot stop. It maximizes exploitation of weaknesses of by appealing to the vanity of players.**

By Jaz McDougall August 19, 2010

Speaking at GDC Europe, Teut Weidemann, design lead on Settlers Online, reckons that to succeed with a Free-To-Play game you need to aggressively target your customers' weaknesses. "We have to bring them in and keep them addicted and make them keep playing." I thought this was the sort of thing you worried about journalists overhearing.

Brandon Sheffield at Gamasutra went to town on this, where developers and industry types have started to chime in on the comments. I'm not surprised. Weidemann relates the sorry predicament of free to play games having to "think about making a fun game and monetizing it at the same time," which he describes as "a huge burden."

What follows is a list of handy hints for exploiting the weaknesses in your customer base so they'll break down and pay, somewhat loosely themed around the seven deadly sins .

Per http://www.deadlysins.com the seven deadly sins are:

1. Pride is excessive belief in one's own abilities that interferes with the individual's recognition of the grace of God. It has been

called the sin from which all others arise. Pride is also known as vanity.

2. Envy is the desire for others' traits, status, abilities, or situation.

3. Gluttony is an inordinate desire to consume more than that which one requires.

4. Lust is an inordinate craving for the pleasures of the body.

5. Anger is manifested in the individual who spurns love and opts instead for fury. It is also known as wrath.

6. Greed is the desire for material wealth or gain, ignoring the realm of the spiritual. It is also called avarice or covetousness.

7. Sloth is the avoidance of physical or spiritual work.

> If you make a grindy game, you can charge the slothful to speed up their leveling process. Put PvP (Player vs. Player) in your game and sell combat advantages to rake in the cash from the wrathful. Offer fancy hats and dresses to exploit your users' vanity. It gets a bit tenuous when he starts talking about the lustful and how they want everything right now, so you should sell them reduced build times for infantry. Whatever floats your boat, I suppose.

> Finally, Weidemann's colleague Christopher Schmitz pipes up with this choice nugget: "Game design is not about game design anymore - now it's about business. If you think you have the same items for this year and next year, you're wrong. You have to change everything like in the Superstore." As one commenter said, "At least he's honest."

Here is a link to the full article:
https://www.pcgamer.com/settlers-online-dev-monetize-all-weakness/

Appendix E:
What Happened to Jack Thompson?
From the website:
The Game of Nerds

Written by: ARMASCRIBE POSTED ON MARCH 19, 2018

Image via BBC.

There was a time when the biggest enemy of gaming was not the industry itself, but a single man. Before the days of micro-transactions, loot boxes and corner cutting conglomerates, the gaming industry was at the mercy of politicians and lawyers who wanted nothing but to gut it entirely. It started in the early 90s, with games like Doom, Night Trap and Mortal Kombat. Horrified parents took to the picket lines and wrote their congressmen to air their growing concerns over the violent media that they were letting their children be exposed to. In the aftermath of one Senate Committee Hearing in 1993, the threat of government-imposed censorship and regulations brought the gaming industry together, and the Entertainment Software Ratings Board (ESRB) was established to implement a rating system. This was not the end of the debate, however. For years to come, an endless stream of politicians and social activists would come out of the woodwork to protest the violence depicted in video games. The most prominent of them was one Jack Thompson. To go up against an entire industry time and time again like Jack Thompson has done throughout the years definitely took guts, and it earned him more than his fair share of infamy. So what ever happened to Jack Thompson?

His story begins in Cleveland, Ohio with him graduating from Cuyahoga Falls High School. He soon after attended Denison University, and later on Vanderbilt University Law School. In 1976, he and his wife moved to Florida, where he spent the next two decades practicing law. His notoriety began during his formative years, well before the video game violence controversy picked up steam in Washington DC. It began in 1988, when he sued Dade County State Attorney Janet Reno for battery for touching him on the shoulder (in response to a question of her sexual orientation). The charge was later dropped, as it was considered a political move on Thompson's part given that he was running for Prosecutor at the time. Reeling from the loss of that election, Thompson would go on to pursue legal action against various Rap artists for obscenity, including 2 Live Crew, N.W.A., Ice-T & MTV.

His first suits against the video game industry began in 1999, during the aftermath of the Heath High School shooting that occurred in West Paducah, Kentucky on December 1st, 1997. 14-year old Michael Carneal had opened fire on a group of students, killing three and injuring five.

Image via Gamasutra

In the subsequent investigation, it was learned that Michael played games like Doom, Quake and Resident Evil, and he frequented numerous Adult websites.

Thompson's suit alleged that Carneal had become desensitized to the violence depicted, and that the games themselves could be considered defective due to the psychological damage inflicted on Carneal. Ultimately, the lawsuit was dismissed on the grounds that Thompson was unable to present any hard evidence to support these claims.

This was not the last time that Thompson would pursue legal action against the developers as a result of violence. It was the beginning of a very long legal career and activism. Over the years, Thompson would file suits against Sony, Take-Two Interactive, Rockstar and even Nintendo, in a legal campaign of what many would describe as very vocal and very public ambulance chases. It should come as no surprise to anyone that anytime any wide-scale forms of violence happened, Jack would be there to speak out against violent entertainment, mostly video games.

He even wrote a book on the subject, "Out of Harm's Way," an autobiography that chronicles many of his legal exploits throughout the years.

His crusade against the gaming industry reached a boiling point in 2005 when he submitted his open letter to the gaming community titled "A Modest Video Game Proposal." In it, he made a proposal: if a game developer were to program a game following a character killing game developers, then he would donate $10,000 to a charity of Take-Two Chairman Paul Eibeler's choosing. A small group of developers known as Thompsonsoft took him up on his offer and released "I'm O.K, a Murder Simulator" in 2006. In it, the protagonist Osaki Kim ("O.K") goes on a murderous rampage across the country to avenge his son, who was killed by a gamer. To the surprise of nobody, Thompson did not fulfill his end of the deal outlined in the proposal, citing that the game didn't meet the requirements of his proposal. Realizing that his end of the bargain wouldn't be met, Mike Krahulik and Jerry Holkins of Penny Arcade fame decided to donate the money in his name. Jack Thompson subsequently attempted to file a police report against them for harassment, though nothing ever came of it. His feud with the industry continued into the latter half of the 2000s with him taking on the gaming community as a whole.

Unsurprisingly, his endeavors had garnered the negative reactions of everyone from average gamers to hardened internet trolls. Because many of his public appearances were televised during the aftermath of many shootings, Thompson had garnered a reputation as a nemesis of the gaming community, oftentimes being compared to an ambulance chaser. The backlash was palpable, though not all gamers were completely at war with him. In 2006, a project dubbed "Flowers for Jack" took donations to send flowers to Thompson's office, along with an open letter attempting to open peaceful talks between Jack and the gaming community. Thompson rejected the gesture and even sent the flowers to his perceived rivals in the gaming industry. His activism continued until 2007, when his frequent lawsuits finally caught up with him.

*In February of that year, the Florida bar moved to disbar him over actions of professional misconduct, as a result of many grievances filed against him throughout his career. According to the **Florida Supreme Court,** Thompson "demonstrated a pattern of conduct to strike out harshly, extensively, repeatedly and willfully to simply try to bring as much difficulty, distraction and anguish to those he considers in opposition to his causes." At the end of a lengthy trial, Thompson was disbarred on September 25th, 2008 and ordered to pay a lengthy fine of $43,675.25.*

Today, Thompson makes his living by teaching civics classes to inmates in Florida, including American History and Constitutional Law classes. While this may sound like a personal defeat to anyone else, to Thompson, his current career path is a victory

Image via Wikipedia.

In an interview with Inverse, Thompson stated that "Watching (mostly poorly educated men) invest themselves in engaging and respectful debates about Constitutional issues—that's the kind of thing that leaves me on the verge of tears."

https://thegameofnerds.com/2018/03/19/what-happened-to-jack-thompson

Appendix F: Shawn's Legacy

From Chapter 7, After Shawn's Death:

At Shawn's wake and funeral, I had people fill out forms, writing about their best memories of him. I then took the completed forms and made a book called "A Legacy to Shawn". I sent the people who shared their memories a copy of the book. I wished Shawn could have read his legacy when he was alive, so he knew how much everyone did like and cared for him. Some of the responses are included below.

Here is the blank form that I used. We are including this as an encouragement for you to use for your own loved one. This legacy has brought me and those who have contributed to it many happy memories and has helped us in our grieving and healing process.

The Legacy of Shawn Woolley

My name is: _____

How I knew Shawn: _____

_____

_____

How I Remember Shawn_____

_____

_____

_____

_____

_____

_____

Shawn Paul Woolley

Born: February 12, 1980
Died: November 20, 2001

Quotes from Shawn's Legacy:

- **Mom - Liz**

How she remembers Shawn: I remember Shawn as being a very unique individual. He was very sensitive. He reminded me a lot of his dad, his grandfather and my brother. They all seem to shy away from people and not quite "fit in".

Shawn was a happy child. He acted like superman – always doing things that were dangerous. He wasn't doing them to show off, he just didn't stop to think that he could get hurt (like jumping down a flight of stairs in one jump, climbing to the top of a 30-foot tree, running next to a moving train). He was in the doctor's office more than all of my other children put together. But he was having fun.

One of Shawn's favorite movies was Night at the Roxbury. After watching it twice in the theater, we ended up buying the movie. Shawn watched it over and over with his younger brother, Tony. They would always imitate Doug and Steve by bopping their heads side to side.

He didn't want to be responsible for himself. He just wanted to play. He would try to be "sneaky" and do things that he knew he wasn't supposed to, yet I would find out about them. He always wondered how I did that. I tried to tell him, "moms know!"

I always worried about Shawn, more than my other 3 children because he had this vulnerability.

When we (my children and I) would get together it was like going to a theater (for me). I just sat and watched the show unfold. What are they going to come up with next? They never disappointed me.

One thing I will always remember about Shawn is that he was my "finder". Whenever I couldn't find something, I would always ask him to help. He never stopped looking, until he found it. To this day, when I can't find something, I ask Shawn to help me find it.

Shawn liked to play and have fun. He was really good with children. He liked being a kid, with the kids. I think he wanted to stay one.

Of course I will miss Shawn. I have to keep telling myself that I don't have to worry about him anymore. I know he is up in heaven with Jesus, and our Mother Mary and he's watching over us with the angels.

- **Brother - Ryan**

How he remembers Shawn: His sense of humor. It was by no means a dark sense of humor. More of a wacky, off-the-wall sense of humor. For example, you could never take just one picture with him in it. You had to take two or three, because he was always goofing off or making a face in one of them or like at family get-togethers, he was always trying to be the class clown. Another thing I remember was his perchance for getting out of house chores. I swear to God that he spent more time and did more work trying to get out of them, then if he would have just done them right away.

I've always felt kind of bad because I felt it was always my job to be his disciplinarian and father figure. And because of this I feel he treated me in accordance. He treated me more like an authority figure then a brother. I always feel like I treated him more like a subordinate than a brother. Shawn, I love you and I'm sorry I didn't treat you as well as I should have sometimes. I will miss you and I pray that God will have mercy on your soul.

(L to R) Shawn, Crystal, Liz, Tony (front) Ryan

- **Sister - Crystal**

How she remembers Shawn: When we were looking through pictures, I remember how Shawn always posed for the camera. When we should have been saying "Cheese!", we were all saying, "Shawn!" trying to get him not to make a funny face. We didn't really like the family snapshots, but we were all laughing by the end, because of his humor.

Shawn really was a sensitive, gentle person. He always took things to heart.

Being asked to write only few stories is hard for me because I have so many. Shawn was my brother and I loved him very much. I hope he can see that. Recently, I would go into his work to see him and he would come out and chat with me. I could see how well everyone liked him.

Recently, I was driving him home and we were talking about how he was doing. He revealed that there was someone that he loved and that touched me. He never talked about that much and I was happy to know that he was capable of feeling love.

He was so proud of his apartment. He was always trying to get me to come by and see his new furniture.

171

Shawn was always the one to be with the cats. He loved them so much. And they always loved him. They were his kitties. They would sleep with him and snuggle upon his bed.

I remember us having a small tight-knit, happy family. We always had good times and laughed. I remember when we got together lately. We would sit and around the living room, tell stories, remember stories and laugh until late night.

One word, SPOONS!

I remember staying up until New Years a couple of years ago. We cleaned up the house after everyone left. I sat down and was writing my resolutions and we sat down and philosophized a bit. He was such a deep thinker that it amazed me.

His millennium – crash plan was funny – ask Ryan exactly what it was. I don't quite remember. He always made us laugh. I will miss him.

- **Brother - Tony**

How he remembers Shawn: Shawn was a nice and caring person. He loved to go bowling with his friends and me. He also loved to build small things and color stuff. He was never selfish. He loved working with his friends. He liked watching movies and TV. He liked when I came over to see him and we played video games together. He liked playing basketball and hockey in our driveway.

- **Grandma Vera**

How she remembers Shawn: Silly, silly, silly when he was with the other cousins and when we took the family pictures. Still being silly!

When he came to my place, we'd play cards. Of course "SPOONS" was his favorite. Remember when he broke the table trying to get a spoon?

I remember when he was going to St. Anne's and how wonderful and caring the teachers would be to Shawn when he would have a seizure and I would go and get him. He was loved by them!

172

- **Uncle Gary and Aunt Maureen**

How they remember Shawn: Aunt Maureen: I remember Shawn growing up, never being able to sit still. He was a skinny kid, and liked to play with his cousins. As he got older he was quieter. After his job at Hardees, he must have finally figured out he liked to eat, and eat he did! He loved his kitties. He liked to act goofy sometimes – I think he took after his Uncle Gary! He loved being on the computer, and liked working at the pizza places! **Uncle Gary –** I remember Shawn – he always wanted to ride the ATV's and Mike and Joe's dirt bikes.

- **Aunt Lorrie**

How she remembers Shawn: Since I don't live up here, I am just going to tell about the last couple of times I saw Shawn. In the summer of 2000, Rebecca, Amanda and I were up here visiting from Alabama. Rebecca was 2 and ½ and Amanda was 10. They took an instant liking to Shawn (he was another kid to play with).

We had bought a rainbow paint kit at the mall and Shawn sat down and painted with us one afternoon. Another time, he went with us to Tony's soccer game. He took Rebecca to the concession stand. As they walked across the field, I remember thinking, "I wish I had a camera". There was big tall Shawn with little Rebecca, hand in hand. **But, that is one picture I will never take.**

- **Grandma Mary**

How she remembers Shawn: Regretting that we were not closer. We lived too much for tomorrow and then tomorrow is gone all too soon.

I remember Shawn at his graduation party, which was very nice and I was happy to know him and have him as a grandson. He will always be remembered with love.

- **Stepdad Greg**

How he remembers Shawn: When I think of Shawn, I think of a person with a wonderful personality, sense of humor and a keen sense of observing the world around him and at the same time, not really able to make sense of it all.

When we rented the motor home and went to the Black Hills, Shawn seemed to love to ride in the bedroom and watch movies. He always kept us entertained with his jokes and imitations of people. His queen wave was a classic. He loved Mount Rushmore, Devil's Tower, the Badlands and Crazy Horse. Elaine's mom and dad came too and really took to Shawn and visa versa. I remember how he always made a face for the camera.

About a year before that we rented a houseboat on Lake Vermillion and Shawn was a joy to be around. He always paid attention to Tony and helped with chores and things that needed to be done.

I remember how thrilled he was about his 1st airplane flight. We went to Washington D.C. and took in all the sights. I think he liked the capital building the best.

Two weeks before he died, Shawn, Tony and I went to a Minnesota Wild hockey game. We went to a restaurant downtown St. Paul. We sat outside by a large heater and had some good food and a couple of beers. Shawn was his normal entertaining self and he really liked the atmosphere of this downtown scene. We went to the game and had a great time. I told him I would get some more tickets and we would go again.

The best times I recall with Shawn, was of Christmas the last few years. We really had fun playing Sequence and watching Sports Bloopers videos.

Shawn was a good man. He was difficult to get to know because he needed his own space and kept people at a distance. And, as often occurs, I have regrets. I wish I would have seeked out his friendship more. I will miss Shawn a lot and I hope that in the future, I can be more of a friend to those in need of one.

174

- **Cousin Michael**

They were the same age. Shawn went to school with him.

How he remembers Shawn: He was a very funny person. If he ever got out of control, I was one of the only people who could calm him down. In school, everybody liked him and got along great with him. Whenever you were around him there was never a dull or boring moment. He always provided entertainment.

One thing that sticks out in my mind the most is he may have always acted goofy, but he is one of the smartest kids I've ever known.

The other thing is, is that when I was with Shawn and on one else was around, we were always having fun, and causing trouble.

- **Cousin Joe**

How he remembers Shawn: I know Shawn not just as a cousin, but also as a friend. If I was ever having a bad day and I saw Shawn, it was like the sun just broke through the clouds. I remember Shawn as **the** funniest person I knew. I remember Shawn always riding our 3-wheelers, snowmobiles and one time he took my mini-bike out for a ride down the road. He held the throttle wide open and never shifted. We had to chase him down with the 4-wheeler so it didn't blow up. Every time I get onto a computer I remember Shawn because I always seen him on a computer. I remember one time he racked up a nice bill on his Mom's computer. (Nice job!)

- **Shawn's second grade teacher Camilla**

How she remembers Shawn: Shawn was such a sweet child. I can remember his shy smile when he was pleased with his work. He tried so hard to do his best.

I taught second grade at St. Anne's for twenty years and in that span of time I knew a lot
of children. Somehow, Shawn stands out as being one of my favorites.

I had a grandson the same age as Shawn and also had epilepsy. Both the boys were blonde and very handsome. What a burden those boys had – knowing they had to take their medications to prevent seizures. My heart went out to them.

- **Brooke went to daycare and school with Shawn.**

How she remembers Shawn: Shawn was always one to make people laugh. He would goof around and that's why the nickname "Woobles" seemed so appropriate.

I also went to church and was confirmed with Shawn.

When we were little, he played on our tee-ball team. It's so memorable because we had tons of fun together and we won 1st at the end of the season. We all went out to the Dallas House for swimming and Shawn would do belly flops into the deep end. Shawn will be missed a lot!

- **Maria was Shawn's friend from childhood.**

How she remembers Shawn: Shawn and I were the only two Osceola kids in our class to attend St. Anne's Catholic school.

Very sweet, caring and loving guy. He would do anything for anyone. I got to know Shawn very well through catechism and he was just a great guy. We got confirmed together. He was a very funny, laughable guy that I enjoyed being around.

- **Nikki was a supervisor of Shawn's when he worked at Hardees**

How she remembers Shawn: I could write forever about Shawn and never have anything negative to say. He has always been very special to me and is probably the most loyal friend I've ever had. I would have done anything for him. I used to have so much fun working with him! He was such a sweet person!

Even though we lost touch after he graduated, he has always been someone I consider my friend. I have never forgotten about him. I miss him very much! I don't think he ever knew how much he meant to me. I can only hope I was as good of a friend to him as he was to me.

- **Kevin worked with Shawn at Papa Murphy's.**

How he remembers Shawn: I will remember Shawn as a funny, easygoing guy. He made Papa Murphy's a fun place to work. One of the things he used to do when he first started was to wear his Dominos hat to work. Anything to stir things up! That was Shawn.

I will always remember Shawn as one of the first reliable employees I had in starting my own business. All the others and I people at Papa Murphy's enjoyed working with him very much.

- **Joy worked with Shawn at Papa Murphy's.**

How she remembers Shawn: I knew two Shawn's. The one I knew when we first started working together to the one who I really knew, the Shawn I loved and cared about. He is the one who greeted me with a hug every morning, who was an encourager to me, he teased me and joked with me all day long and I couldn't even begin to write the stories about the things that happened that we would laugh so hard about. So many little "inside jokes" we had "the power of cheese" was one phrases that could get Shawn going. I would sing to him and drive him nuts but he would eventually laugh and the next thing we might catch him dancing or singing too. He spent time at our home an enjoyed the kids from our youth group who hung out at our house. My daughter Alicia who he loved to mis-say her name whenever he talked to her (she too worked with Shawn). Of course being old enough to be Shawn's mom, I would mother him, feed him and we had many great talks. I will miss Shawn. Please call if there is anything I can ever do.

- **Sam worked with Shawn at Papa Murphy's and they attended Alpha at his church together.**

How he remembers Shawn: I remember Shawn as a co-worker and a friend. When Shawn worked at a task he would stay at it until completion, without complaining. He had a great sense of humor and was often telling jokes or laughing. He had the best laugh; just hearing it made me want to laugh with him. I remember when Shawn was goofy, too. If a song he knew would come on the radio, he would sing along or dance. He was hilarious! We went out for lunch or dinner several times. I remember going to Happy Chinn Garden, Denny's and every Thursday we went to Faith Community Church for Alpha. We had some great conversations. Alpha is a program for people who have questions about God. At the start, there was a meal provided, which Shawn and I ate together. He had many questions about God. Mostly he would just listen and think about everything. He had a great mind and I know he wanted to work with computers in the future.

I can honestly say that Shawn was a friend of mine and that I am blessed because of him.

We hung out together at my house, at his apartment and at his friend's house. He was really likeable, thoughtful, funny yet quiet guy and he will be missed.

I thank God for Shawn and I pray that anyone who reads this will seek the peace and love that only comes from the Lord.

I love you Shawn - sorry I never got to say goodbye. – Sam

- **Nathan worked with Shawn at Papa Murphy's.**

How he remembers Shawn: I remember Shawn as a big Teddy bear. When we would work together we would tell each other jokes and make jokes about the other workers.

He was hard to get to know at first but after the ice was broken it was easy. I have a lot of good memories about Shawn. When I would drop him off after work we would go garage sailing for stuff for his new place.

He spent Easter at my sister's house. He had the hardest time finding his basket, but in the end he found it.

I had to break him in with lots of hugs. One of the last times I saw him, he ran up to me and lifted me off the ground and gave me a bear hug.

One of the funny memories that I have of Shawn is when we were at work. He would try to pour oil into a spray bottle and I would make him laugh. He would laugh so hard he would spill all over the floor. Then he would try to rub it into the concrete floor with his shoe. I have great memories of Shawn. He was a great friend n and a good guy all around. He will be missed.

- **Cassie worked with Shawn at Papa Murphy's. She and her husband and family became good friends with him.**

How she remembers Shawn: Shawn was hard to get to know at first, but he came around. I looked forward to working with him. He was a hard worker and a lot of fun to be around. I'll remember him trying to find his Easter basket – we played hot and cold and eventually, he found it. He talked about cooking, computers, getting a car and his shake maker. We had fun helping him shop for his new place – he was so excited and proud.

He was friendly and loving and eventually liked hugs. It was a pleasure to get to know Shawn and become his friend. We will miss him very much.

**1998 - Shawn's graduation picture by Cascade Falls
in Osceola, WI.**

Appendix G: Events of Shawn's Life, Chronologically

1980 – February 12 - Shawn was born, St. Croix Falls, WI.

1986 – July - Shawn started having grand mal seizures. Was diagnosed with epilepsy and was prescribed Depakote.

1990 – August - Shawn joined school band and played saxophone.

1992 – September - Shawn was diagnosed with ADD (attention deficit disorder) and was prescribed Cylert.

1993 – September - Shawn went on vacation to Washington D.C. with his stepdad, Greg, Elaine, and his younger brother, Tony

1995 – Spring - Shawn got his first job at the local Hardees in Osceola, WI.

1996 – Summer - Shawn went on a ten-day vacation to South Dakota with his brother Tony, stepdad Greg, Elaine and Elaine's parents, Lucille and Bob.

1996 – November - Shawn went on a TEC (Teens Encounter Christ) retreat for church.

1997 – April - Shawn made his confirmation at the St. Patrick's Catholic Church in Centuria, WI.

1998 – May - Shawn graduated from high school.

1998 - August - Shawn started school at St. Paul Technical Institute, for graphic arts.

1999 - January - Quit Vo-tech school for Graphic Arts.

1999 - Spring – Shawn got a job at Menards – worked there through the summer.

2000 – February - On his 20th birthday, Shawn purchased his first MMORPG (massive multiplayer online role-playing game) video game called Everquest and started playing it on the Vallon Zek server.

2000 - April - Shawn moved out to a place of his own and was promoted to Assistant Manager at Domino's

2000 - July 2 - Shawn had grand mal seizure. Went to work. Quit his job.

2000 - July – September - Shawn played Everquest, day and night. Did not get a job. Was evicted in September.

2000 – September - Moved back to Liz's home. Went to see a therapist.

2000 - December 22 - Liz made Shawn leave her home.

2000 - December 27 - Liz was able to get Shawn help from St. Croix county, thanks to a miracle.

2001 – January - Shawn was accepted to Long Term Support program group home.

2001 - February - Shawn received the diagnosis of major depression, dysthymia, passive dependency, schizoid personality characteristics. (From page 45.)

2001 - May - Started a new job at Papa Murphy's pizza.

2001 - June - Shawn moved in to his own apartment.

2001 – July - Shawn's older brother Ryan got married. Shawn came to the wedding. Shawn did not stay for the whole event.

2001 – July - Shawn had a seizure and ended up in the Emergency Room at local hospital.

2001 - August - Shawn got his own computer.

2001 – September - Shawn disconnected his phone.

2001 – September - Shawn's first nephew, Zachariah was born.
2001 - 9/11 happened.

2001 – October - Shawn stopped communication with his family.

2001 - October 31 - Shawn came to Liz's house for Halloween and the caseworker informed her that he had stopped taking his medications.

2001 – November 1- Liz contacted Shawn's caseworker and she informed Liz, that Shawn had not been to his Doctor appointments - since August.

2001 – November - Shawn went to Timberwolves game with little brother Tony and his stepdad Greg.

2001 – November 11 - Shawn refused to go to the annual family "harvest" meal at grandma Vera's house..

2001 – Tuesday, November 13 - Shawn purchased a rifle.

2001 – November 15 - Shawn's boss told Liz that he'd not come to work that week.

2001 – November 16 - Liz went to Shawn's place (Friday before Thanksgiving.) This was the last time Liz saw Shawn alive.

2001 – November 22 - Liz found Shawn sitting at his computer with the Everquest login-screen on it - dead.

2001 – November 26 - Funeral for Shawn held at St. Patrick's Church in Hudson, WI.

REFERENCES

- *Letting God* by A. Philip Parham

- Since Shawn's death, there have been many more deaths, as a direct result of these games. Here are the ones we are aware of: http://www.olganon.org/forums/gaming-related-deaths

- **20/20 ABC TV: Digital Addiction** Excellent show about Gaming Addiction. Even has MRI's of gamers brains, before and after treatment....
  https://www.youtube.com/watch?v=Ytte2C1rdiU

- The Digitally Compulsive Family by John Najar

- The Reason for My Hope by Billy Graham

- ***National Suicide Prevention Lifeline:*** 800-273-8255

RESOURCES

- *On-Line Gamers Anonymous® at www.olganon.org*
- *OLGAnon Youtube Channel:*
  https://www.youtube.com/playlist?list=PL2f2Jidau8uhvIOJxT
  LNHjSXgSe3ALSI8
- Also, go to **YouTube** and search for Gaming Addicts or Game
  Addiction. There are many videos created by addicts
  themselves, about this latest addiction.
- *Plugged In,* by Terry Waite
- *Out of Harm's Way* by Jack Thompson
- *Born to Win*: *Transactional Analysis With Gestalt*
  Experiments by Muriel James
- *Hooked on Games*: *The Lure and Cost of Video Game and*
  Internet Addiction by Andrew Doan
- *Cyber Junkie*: *Escape the Gaming and Internet Trap* Written
  by Kevin Roberts; Published by the Hazelden/Betty Ford
  Foundation
- *Fast Lane to Heaven*: *Celestial Encounter that Changed My*
  Life by Ned Dougherty
- *The Purpose Driven Life* by Rick Warren
- *Jesus Calling* by Sarah Young
- Readings for Recovery -
  http://www.olganon.org/forums/readings-recovery
- Videos for recovery - http://www.olganon.org/forums/videos-recovery
- Books about video gaming addiction -
  http://www.olganon.org/forums/books-about-gaming-addiction
- Videos about video gaming addiction -
  http://www.olganon.org/forums/videos-about-gaming-addiction
- Teens Encounter Christ (TEC)
- Wilderness Camps
- Word of Life Camp in New York

Made in the USA
Middletown, DE
03 May 2022